THE WIT AND HUMOU

The Wit and Humour of Dáil Éireann

PADRAIC O'FARRELL

THE MERCIER PRESS
CORK and DUBLIN

The Mercier Press Limited
4 Bridge Street, Cork
24 Lower Abbey Street, Dublin 1

British Library Cataloguing in Publication Data
O'Farrell, Padraic
   The wit and humour of Dáil Éireann.
   1. Ireland, *Oireachtas, Dáil* — Anecdotes, facetiae, satire, etc.
   I. Title
   328.417'072'0207   JN1468

ISBN 0-85342-760-7

To Naomi and Barry

ACKNOWLEDGEMENT

All extracts quoted in this book are from *Diospóireachtaí Páirliminte
– Tuairisg Oifigiúil* (Parliamentary Debates – Official Report) and are
reproduced with the permission of the Controller, Stationery Office.

Printed by Litho Press Co., Midleton, Co. Cork.

Contents

Foreword

A study of Dáil Éireann's Parliamentary Debates cannot but impress even the most cynical observer. This is true particularly of the early years of the state. Here were men unaccustomed to the ways of parliament and unversed in the nuances of enacting legislation, yet setting about the mammoth task of bringing order out of chaos in a vigorous and forthright manner.

When I set about compiling this book I hoped that my research would unearth an occasional *bon mot* which would provide me with the opportunity of passing humorous comment or satirical barb. It soon became evident that there was a wealth of material which would be better presented as uttered. Explanatory or whimsical asides would only blur the brightness of the parliamentary particle!

But would it be right and proper to smile at the expressions of our early Teachtaí Dála, most of them now passed away? Although still a young nation, we have matured in many ways. A great test of maturity is the ability to laugh at oneself. In the following pages, the nation is under test. Possessing a sense of humour towards a subject pays it tribute. A successful man recently retired from an onerous state appointment once reminded me that being devoid of a sense of humour was a disability; like being without a limb or speech or hearing.

So let not those who are humourless venture further in this assessment of national maturity. After all, we want the nation we love to pass its test and come through with flying colours. Let us remember the words of Abraham Lincoln: 'The legitimate object of government is to do for a community of people whatever they need to have done. . .' and who says we don't need our parliamentarians – even those no longer serving or with us – to give us a laugh in these depressing times?

Padraic O'Farrell

1. In the Beginning. . .

The early days of Dáil Éireann were spent in serious deliberations. People unaccustomed to parliamentary procedures set out to establish a proper forum for discussing the affairs of the nation. Items for debate were controversial and needed sensitive handling. Nevertheless, the word 'laughter' in brackets appeared occasionally. The debate on the Treaty on 19 December 1921 provides an appropriate opening example.
Alderman W. T. Cosgrave (Minister for Local Government): If a decision on the matter were already given at the Secret Session, are we to be like a Board of Guardians, passing a resolution one day, and rescinding it the next day? *(laughter)*. . .

*   *   *   *   *

Ald. Liam De Roiste: . . . Take for the moment that the English troops – the English armed forces – are out of this country, and I put up a tricolour on Dublin Castle, I will dare anyone to take it down *(laughter)*. Now we have got a flag. What we have been told here is this: that if Arthur Griffith puts it up on Dublin Castle there are people here who would go and take it down.
Mr R. Mulcahy: We will take the Castle down *(laughter)*.

*   *   *   *   *

The practice of spelling out the laughter in reports soon ceased but on Thurday 5 January 1922 there occurred what may well have been the first parliamentary airing of a practical joke.
Alderman Cosgrave: On a point of order I would like to bring this matter before the house. Yesterday I was informed that one of the principal business houses in this city received this letter:

Sinn Féin Headquarters,
6 Harcourt Street, Dublin.
January 3, 1922

Dear Sirs,
    We have found that it will not be possible for us to obtain a Union Jack of sufficient size in the event of its being

necessary for us to display one at the end of the session of Dáil Éireann when the Treaty will, in all probability, have been ratified. We are anxious to comply with all the necessary courtesies, and propose to hoist the Union Jack beside the Green Flag on the University Building as soon as the result of the discussion is known. We would be grateful if you would give the bearer your largest flag. We will, of course, return it to you as soon as the one which we have ordered arrives.

We are, dear Sirs, Yours faithfully,
M. Whelan, *Secretary*,
Decoration Committee,
Irish Free State.

We are here by the courtesy and consent of the University authorities of which President de Valera is Chancellor.
Mr P. O'Keefe: I am Chief Executive Officer in 6 Harcourt Street, and that is a forgery. If never came from 6 Harcourt Street.

* * * * *

Minister for Defence (General Mulcahy): I am aware that bicycles have been commandeered by our troops in Ballinasloe. They were taken and are being retained as a matter of military necessity. . .

* * * * *

Mr D. J. Gorey: . . . Will a vote of want of confidence passed in the Dáil remove any one of those Ministers? If that were so I would be satisfied; but if there are going to be lengthy investigations and inquiries and wire-pulling, I do not like it. . .

* * * * *

A statement from Mr Gorey pre-dated John F. Kennedy's famous words.
Mr D. J. Gorey: Some people have teachers on the brain. Residences for the whole of them, built by the Board of Works. . . The practice in Leinster is that people in the district get together, put the money down, and build the residence. Try and help yourself, and do not be asking the Nation always to help you – always going around with the hat.

* * * * *

Mr Darrell Figgis: I notice under the heading A it says 'Law Officers'. I am not quite clear what may be included in that. I understood there was only one Law Officer technically so called. Who exactly would be included in that term?

The President: There is one Law Officer; there is an assistant Law Officer, and I do not know but the sum includes some Law Officers that we may have got delivery of. I am not sure but I will enquire if the Deputy wishes.

Mr Darrell Figgis: What exactly does that phrase mean 'that we got delivery of', delivery by post or delivery by pantechnicon?

The President: They came in on their feet, so far as I know, and they remained on their feet.

*   *   *   *   *

Thomas O'Connell asked the Minister for Defence if he was aware that in spite of his statement in the Dáil, on 11 October 1922, that instructions had been issued for receipts to be given for all bicycles commandeered in Ballinasloe, no receipt had yet been given to Mr Thomas Brogan, of Ballaghadereen, whose bicycle was commandeered on 2 October by a flying column under Captain Mitchell of Boyle, and whether, in view of the fact that application was made on four occasions from 12 October 1922 to 8 January 1923, without any result, he would cause Mr Brogan's bicycle to be returned to him, if it is still fit for return, or, if it is not, to cause compensation to be given therefor.

*   *   *   *   *

Mr Milroy: I would like to ask the President if we are to infer. . . that the Minister for Industry and Commerce is also the Minister for Fashions. . .

*   *   *   *   *

Arguments about summer and winter times have been with us for a long time, but Mr Gorey's contribution was unique.

Mr Gorey: Before offering any observations on the Bill I want to extend my sympathy to the Minister who introduced this measure. . . Of course, we cannot blame our modern legislators. They are attempting to do something that was never done before. They are attempting to do something that the Creator never intended should be done. It seems to be that this phase of modern legislation aims at out-doing the Creator. They are trying to show that they are cleverer and know more than the Lord did when he created the world.

It is argued that the alteration would be good for some. Perhaps it would be good for Bank officials and others of that sort. In my opinion, one of the reasons that we have taken up this is because, as a people, we have been fond of taking up cant phrases and cheap inventions. A cant phrase is not out three or four days in England when it is in vogue in Ireland. We are fond of imitations without considering whether the things we imitate are right or wrong, or are likely to be successful. . .

Mr W. L. Cole: . . . workers in towns are more in favour of Summer Time than the people in the country. . . The people in the West of Ireland would be going out before 4 o'clock.

Mr Gorey: The people in the West of Ireland are out all night.

Mr O'Connell: They are going home at that time. . .

Mr Gorey: As to this question of the milking of the cows, I want to emphasise that, as a matter of fact, the cows are milked in their sleep.

Mr O'Connell: This is why they give so much water.

* * * * *

Mr Darrell Figgis: . . . the question was put as to whether the Governor-General, in addition to getting these quarterly payments. . . was to receive a certain pension: that it was a pensionable office. . . I mean that he receives £10,000 a year, and that he signs certain necessary documents before participating in his punch at night, and sleeps thereafter, and that that is the end of the liability.

An Ceann Comhairle: I think Deputy Figgis is wandering absolutely from this amendment.

The President: The memory of punch always makes him wander.

* * * * *

Professor Magennis: . . . the standard that is applicable with regard to the individual spectator is not applicable with regard to the whole crowded audience, particularly mixed audiences, audiences that witness in the same city Dante's *Inferno* and Charlie Chaplain –

Mr Darrell Figgis: Who is Charlie Chaplain?

Professor Magennis: Who is Dante?

* * * * *

Mr Blythe: . . . in the case of a large number of people, you must have all necessary powers, you might say summary powers. . .
Mr Darrell Figgis: They are not summary powers, they are 'wintry' powers.

* * * * *

The President: . . . Just imagine an unarmed colleague walking into a man of the fierce demeanour of Deputy Figgis and saying: 'I am going to take your library' . . .

* * * * *

The President: . . . The most ardent tea drinker that I have ever come across has never raised any particular objection to the tax imposed on tea. Deputies beyond, I should say, if you were to question them very closely, would admit that it was an article of diet which cannot be very well recommended, and, if we reverted to commodities used in this country before the introduction of tea, that it would be in the interest of persons affected who would consume these particular things.
Mr Darrell Figgis: Whiskey.

* * * * *

Mr W. O'Brien: Does the Minister consider that it is improper that a military officer should carry on his duty as a shopkeeper at the same time side by side, and is he aware that this officer is to be seen frequently milking his cows, in full uniform?

* * * * *

Professor Magennis: . . . Could not Crossley tenders, covered in, be employed in country districts, and, as I pointed out, bring children from the outlying parts dryshod, warm and comfortable, to properly equipped schools?

* * * * *

Mr Davin: . . . it will cost him more to keep an Irish terrier than it would to make a two shillings and sixpence a week provision for the education of his family.
Mr Gorey: It would all depend on whether he is ill-bred or not. Mongrels eat too much.

* * * * *

Professor Magennis: . . . One of my earliest recollections is a political rhyme which went as follows:

> Feeble counsels weakly planned;
> Funk that fears the traitor band;
> Foster in supreme command:
> Feeble, funky Foster.

That was the Die-hard's version of the three F's. Here we have the three F's resuscitated. I thought I wept over their tomb — fixity of tenure, fair rent and free sale. This is another of the usual devices of the reviewer of books. If he does not complain of the title, he complains that the book was not about something else. . .

* * * * *

Mr Davin: The Press is not here, and I am speaking quite frankly. I want to assure you in the absence of the Press that I am not a professional politician.

* * * * *

Dr White: . . . crops very suitable for agricultural pursuits would be many of them medicinal plants.
Mr Gorey: Scutch grass.

* * * * *

Professor Magennis: . . . I will bear in mind what happened in. the case of the clergyman who was getting a *locum tenens,* or a local demon as it is popularly called. The new clergyman asked how long he was expected to preach and the answer was; 'well there is a feeling in this congregation that there are no souls saved after the first half hour'.

* * * * *

Seoirse de Bhulb: I am rather like the lady who was so bothered by her admirers that she was recommended by her medical adviser to go on board ship to get rid of them. When she got on board ship she found that the captain and the crew gave her so much annoyance that she had to jump overboard to get rid of them. . .

* * * * *

Sean Mac Giobuin: There is a well-known motor car on the market. It is called the Dodge. People journeying up and down the country have noticed artful greengrocers flashing by in these luxurious conveyances. The green producer has, however, to be content with the ass and cart. Slightly altered, the old rhyme would go near to mirroring the position:

> There was an old prophecy found in a Lodge,
> That Ireland would be ruled by an Ass and a Dodge,
> Now, that old prophecy has come to pass,
> The Profiteer is the Dodge, the Producer the Ass.

*   *   *   *   *

Mr Milroy: . . . This is not a question for the Minister for Home Affairs to be a thought reader, and to be able to anticipate that, in six months time, a certain thought will pass through Deputy Lyons's head. I wonder does anybody anticipate that such a phenomenon is likely to happen. . .

*   *   *   *   *

Mr Hogan: The war lasted from 1914 to 1918. I would like to ask how many hens would lay £5 worth of eggs per year. One good hen would do it.
Mr Gorey: The Minister's hens. I want to put in a claim for sitting on the Minister's eggs. I have first claim.

*   *   *   *   *

Mr Milroy: Deputy Gorey always reminds me of a blend of Ancient Pistol and Don Quixote. He makes a terrific noise which means nothing. He is tilting, like Don Quixote, at windmills. This is one of his windmills. It is quite clear that the Deputy knows very little about this matter. Otherwise we would have been treated to a much longer and much more frantic discourse. . .

*   *   *   *   *

Mr Walsh: . . . The only application received for a licence to sell stamps has come from a shopkeeper whose premises are licensed for this sale and consumption of intoxication liquor. . .

*   *   *   *   *

Mr Colohan: ... The birch can be used by a practised flogger to do considerable damage to a man's back and leave the bones bare.

Mr Darrell Figgis: ... I venture to say in the most quiet and emphatic way that I am not in the habit of making either faked or excited statements in this Dail. They may be inaccurate, but they will not be inaccurate to my knowledge. ...

* * * * *

Deputy Gorey spoke of 'getting in the thin edge of the wedge' and 'giving the wedge a foothold'. This prompted the remark:

Mr O'Connell: ... Apart from the fact that wedges have not feet, the thin end of the wedge is in already. . .

* * * * *

The monorail from Listowel to Ballybunion received mention.

The President: ... here is..., I believe, a remarkable contribution to railway road construction in the South.

A Deputy: The Lartigue.

The President: With rolling stock of a very unique kind.

Mr Johnson: Very much rolling.

* * * * *

General Mulcahy told Mr Connor Hogan that a decision would shortly be reached in connection with a car commandeered by the Army at Ennis on 9 August 1922.

Mr Connor Hogan: Will the Minister give us the Departmental interpretation of the significance of the word 'shortly'. Does it mean in the course of a few days, or in the course of a few weeks, or a few months or a few years, the latter of which, relatively speaking would represent only an atom of time in the cycle of eternity?

* * * * *

Mr Milroy: ... Peter the Great, on one occasion discussing lawyers, said: 'There were two lawyers in my Dominions; I hanged one of them'. I must say, when I perused this report, my disposition towards professors of political economy was much the same as that of Peter the Great towards lawyers. However, I suppose it is not practical politics to translate that disposition into actualities, and I suppose it is not even possible to bring them within the meaning of the Minister for Home Affairs' 'Flogging' Bill. . .

* * * * *

Mr Darrell Figgis: . . . If anybody says to me that porter and stout are not food, I shall refute any such critic with the complaint of an old lady in the Coombe, who asked how it was possible to continue these times with the price of food at 8d. per pint. . .

* * * * *

After lengthy discussion on the Housing (Building Facilities) Bill 1924 Mr Morrissey made an apt remark.
Mr Morrissey: A Leas-Chinn Chomhairle, I would like to point out that you have not a House.

* * * * *

The President: . . . Deputy Lyons, I think, mentioned something about a plum tree. I would like to know if the deputy would submit himself to the particular operation he mentioned – improving the rest of his body at the expense of his head. I am afraid the deputy could not afford anything off the top.
Mr Lyons: On a point of explanation, I think I can answer that question. If I let my hair grow long enough I must get it removed if I am to look well.

* * * * *

Pádraig Ó hÓgáin (An Clár) asked the Minister for Home Affairs if it is proposed to compensate Mr John Conlan, Kilmorane, Darrah, Ennis, in respect of a jennet, his property, seized by National troops at New Hall, Ennis, in June 1923, and if, in consideration of the fact that Mr Conlan is a labourer having no means of support but his wages, he will favourably consider the position with a view to compensating him.

* * * * *

During a debate on the Policy of the Minister for Local Government on 5 March 1924, Mr McKenna told how, at a meeting of Westmeath County Council 'a body of men entered the Council Chamber, and they kicked tables, chairs and everything upside down.' He asked: 'Is that fair or is it constitutional Government?'
Mr Corish: It is constitutional starvation?

Mr Egan: (referring to Tullamore) It is a town in the middle of an agricultural district, and that is as near as I can get to a definition of an agricultural district.
(Later)
. . . In the town of Tullamore, which I come from, and which is a fairly important industrial district –
Mr Davin: I thought it was an agricultural district a few moments ago?
Mr Egan: Well, I am discussing a different matter now.

* * * * *

Mr Darrell Figgis: . . . I believe it would have been very much better if the course that seemed to be likely to take place when the late Minister for Industry and Commerce spoke yesterday had taken place according to its original intention. . . .
The President: May I put the Deputy right? I think he has made a constitutional mistake. He said 'the late Minister'. The Minister is still alive, thank God. . .

* * * * *

Mr Wolfe: . . . I think it is a futile thing to think that because women have the vote they can ever be put, in all cases, on equal terms with men. It has never been suggested that they should be asked to serve in the Army. I do not think our Minister for Defence has issued instructions for recruiting amongst the ladies, and hitherto they have not been asked to serve in the Navy.

* * * * *

Mr Wilson: Will the Minister say did the County Court Judge in this case do any other duty while he was idle, or did he take a holiday?
Mr Blythe: I think he played golf.
Mr Gorey: Was he receiving a salary for playing golf? I hope he is giving satisfaction to the state on the links.

* * * * *

Mr Lynch: . . . Deputy Hewat thought that the Department is apparently being made a grandmother for fisheries.
Mr O'Connell: A milch cow.

* * * * *

Mr Desmond Fitzgerald: Before the adjournment is moved the President has asked me to announce that General O'Duffy has reported to him that two Lewis guns and 500 rounds of ammunition were handed in today in Tipperary.

Mr Heffernan: Might I ask if that is Tipperary County or Tipperary Town?

Mr Fitzgerald: My information is Tipperary.

Mr Heffernan: We are a long way from there.

*   *   *   *   *

Mr Burke: . . . If there is no evidence of age there can be no question of a pension.

Mr Darrell Figgis: Even though the applicant was born in the year of the Big Wind.

*   *   *   *   *

Major Cooper: What is the use of having a plough if you have no horses to pull it? If your horses or your donkeys are taken away and seized, what is the use of having a plough?

Mr Heffernan: The neighbours are always very kind.

*   *   *   *   *

Postmaster General: . . . I have no doubt myself, if this House determines that the Post Office must do the showman, must differentiate between rival organ-grinders, rival tenors and people of that kind, and even rival politicians who want to get control and preferential treatment, we will be able to do it; but we will do it at a price, and it will be a very dear price.

Mr Gorey: Hear, Hear.

Postmaster General: I am very sorry to see that Deputy Gorey 'hear hear's' a forecast which is likely to rape the finance of the nation.

Mr Gorey: I 'hear hear' the idea that we would be able to do something right if we tried.

*   *   *   *   *

The President: . . . while we might possibly say that it is time to take the Seanad out of the Antique Furniture Room of the Museum, we ourselves are in a theatre.

An Ceann Comhairle: A theatre devoted to high art.

*   *   *   *   *

Mr A. McCabe: . . . I believe that if ever there is a naval war, Ireland and Irish seas are going to be the cockpits of the world. Therefore, I say that this subject of territorial waters is of the very deepest interest. . .

* * * * *

Mr Gorey: I am sorry to disappoint Deputy Davin, in not rising before. I am even a closer sticker to my seat than he is.

* * * * *

Mr Gorey: This resolution deals with dried fruits.
Major Cooper: Is it in accordance with precedent that we could smuggle through motor-cars disguised as raisins?

* * * * *

Major Cooper: I cannot help thinking that these duties are a backward step and are mistaken, particularly in so far as the small musical instruments and things like gramophone records are concerned.
Mr Johnson: And mouth organs?
Major Cooper: I thank Deputy Johnson. He has been attending a congress of his colleagues across the water, and he probably heard mouth organs.
Mr Johnson: Tin whistles.

* * * * *

Major Cooper: Before we vote on this I should very much like Deputy Gorey to tell me what is the raw material of jam. It is one of the greatest mysteries we have.
Mr Wilson: Turnips.
Mr Gorey: Mangolds and turnips.

* * * * *

Major Cooper: My information, such as it is, is that we are overstocked with bottles in this country.
A Deputy: Empty ones.

* * * * *

Mr Milroy: . . .I can imagine Deputy Lyons, who is not in the Dáil at present, but whose name occurs to me as the only Deputy that I heard giving statistics as to the number of his family, after being away from home for a considerable time coming back to find his children starving for want of food. He would not say, 'Well, now, I will experiment on one, perhaps the weakest and sickliest of the lot, and try a little food on him. If it is beneficial to him, and if he recovers, I will try it on the rest. If he dies it will be proof that feeding the child is not going to save it from the results of starvation.' He may point to his neighbour, Deputy Gorey's children on the other side, who are well fed and healthy, and say, 'It is not because they are fed they are so healthy, but in spite of the fact that they are well fed; you must try and become efficient in getting used to starvation and show that this theory about being fed is something preposterous.' . . .

* * * * *

Mr Johnson: I would like to support the contention of Deputy Cooper regarding gramophone records and needles. I would put in the plea that a gramophone record is not a part of the musical instrument.
Mr Blythe: It is an accessory, I believe.
Mr Johnson: Yes, an accessory, in the same way as wind is an accessory to a cornet, and if the Minister is proposing to put a tax on the wind he will have a rather considerable job. I remember many years ago it was a fairly common practice to play music from an instrument made up of a comb and a piece of thin paper. Will the Minister consider these to be a musical instrument when combined, and will he therefore put a tax on the paper or on the comb? . . .

* * * * *

Mr Walsh, Minister for Posts and Telegraphs: . . . the question of reverting to the previous arrangement whereby the use of one stamp form would suffice for more than one dog owned by the same person is being taken up with the Ministry of Home Affairs.
Mr Gorey: Arising out of that question, is it a fact that the Minister wants to put in operation the old old maxim, that 'every tub must stand on its own bottom', and that in this case every dog must stand on his own stamp?

* * * * *

Concerning Mr Burke, Minister for Local Government and Public Health, this was said:

Professor O'Sullivan: May I point out that on Friday we spent about an hour considering as to whether we were to burk the discussion, and I suggest now that we do not spend an hour discussing Burke.

* * * * *

Mr Hewat: . . . Now, what does most damage to the roads? Is it a petrol-driven vehicle or a steam lorry? I will ask Deputy Gorey to say which does more harm? Steam motors do not use any petrol, and is the steam motor perambulating the country with a double weight of chassis and propelled by another fuel, to go scot free?
Mr Gorey: No, we will deal with that.
Mr Hewat: How then?
Professor O'Sullivan: Tax coal.

* * * * *

Mr Johnson: I suggest that if the Minister would inquire he would find that in nine cases out of ten it is from the producers' end that the eggs are dirtied.

* * * * *

Mr Daly: . . . Alas, we are asked not to taste a tint of drink on St Patrick's Day. Our fathers would turn in the grave if they heard it. Many of them got their heads smashed on St Patrick's Day, and it would not be a Patrick's Day unless they came home half 'boosed'. All those time-honoured customs are to be put aside to please the Pioneers, the people who have a big banner, with Pussyfoot drawn out on it. I do not like to say anything against the Pioneers, because I am a kind of Pioneer myself. I may as well say that, because some Deputy may fling a taunt at me, 'Why don't you have a drink yourself?' I drank my own share of it.
(Later)
Mr Darrell Figgis: A friend of mine in the country a short time ago had occasion to employ a man cutting his turf, and entertaining him at lunch thought he would try him with a bottle of claret to see how the taste would agree with him. The man drank his bottle of claret, and he drank a second bottle of claret, and when he was asked how he savoured that for a drink he replied: 'Well, it is not too bad a drink but you know, sir, it is very tedious.' . . .

* * * * *

Mr O'Higgins: . . . Such liquids as water, tea, coffee or minerals do not count in the vocabulary of the clubmen, if we are to believe all that has been said here.

Mr Johnson: Especially golf club-men.

Mr O'Higgins: . . . The point has been made that for a few weeks in summer golf may, with good sight and good luck be played up to 9.30 or after it.

The fact is – and everyone knows it – that if things went on as they have been going on, the tendency would be that these clubs would become less and less golf clubs and more and more just late-night drinking dens, from which people would go home uproarious in the small hours of the morning.

Mr Gorey: They might not come home at all.

Mr O'Higgins: Killing Deputy Gorey's stock, maybe, with their motor-cars on the roadside on their way home. . .

*   *   *   *   *

Major Cooper: Now, I think that if there was a great future for a whole milk and cream trade in the British market the Danes, who are active and enterprising farmers, would have discovered and captured it.

Mr Johnson: They are a further distance away.

Major Cooper: Yes, but there is another factor which affects both them and ourselves, and which Deputy Johnson seems to have forgotten, and that is that both in their case and in ours there is a sea passage, and you cannot guarantee that the sea will be smooth at any season of the year. I venture to think that a wholesaler in England hoping to buy whole milk or cream from this country or Denmark would be disappointed if, when opening his cans, he found butter. That is what would happen very often if we embarked on this trade. It is a precarious enterprise, and not even Deputy Johnson can command the movements of the sea. I think he suggested that we would need a special apparatus, but unless you had a special arrangement, like the hanging gardens of Babylon, which would hang in the ship and not be susceptible to motion, it could not be done.

Mr Johnson: I wonder if the Deputy ever sat on an ass's cart carrying milk to a creamery?

*   *   *   *   *

Mr Esmonde: . . .The President is Commander-in-Chief and Minister for Defence, but I doubt if the President could defend Dalkey Island against an invasion. How many guns has he got? I am informed that we have only four guns which are capable of going off at all.

*　　*　　*　　*　　*

Risteard Ó Malochatha asked the Minister for Defence if he would state what is a Dry Canteen.

Minister for Defence (The President): A Dry Canteen in a barracks is a saloon in which are sold hot and cold foods and non-alcoholic drinks, including tea, coffee and cocoa and other luxuries and necessaries usually purchased by soldiers. . .

*　　*　　*　　*　　*

Mr O'Higgins: . . . The amendment is simply a wedge whereby a completely different vista is opened up. The thing takes this complexion: two people meet in the street and one says: 'Can we get a drink today?' The other replies: 'Oh, yes, you can, under the law, provided you have a meal.' The first says: 'Then we will risk the meal,' and they go in and order their drink and have a biscuit or a sandwich or one is before them on a plate for a very long time, and the consumption of drink would be out of all proportion to the consumption of food. I have a kind of objection in a personal way to taking responsibility for legislation that simply opens up absurd possibilities of that kind, and I oppose the amendment on those grounds.

Major Cooper: The Minister's argument is as mouldy as his sandwich. . . .

(Later)

Mr Gorey: I can understand a customer going unto a public-house with a shilling or two to spend. I can understand him also going into a butcher's shop. As the Minister for Justice has said, liquor is a very peculiar type of goods, and the difference between it and other commodities can be shown by an illustration. If a man goes into a butcher's shop and asks for 1½ or 2 lbs of meat, and consumes it on the premises, very well, but I cannot understand if he then says, 'Give me another 1½ or 2 lbs!' I can very well understand the position of a man going into a public-house and buying a half-pint or a pint of whiskey, and when that is consumed asking – as is the most natural thing in the world – for more. . . .

(Later)
Mr Daly: . . . Stout and beer, as far as making one drunk is concerned, will run a dead heat.
(Later)
Mr O'Higgins: . . . Goldsmith's lines might be adapted, and we might speak of
    A land to hastening ills a prey,
    Where pubs accumulate and men decay.

*   *   *   *   *

Mr Gorey: Water may be perfectly pure and at the same time may not be good water. For instance, poison might be good, but it might not be particularly good when mixed with butter. I think the word 'good' is better than the word 'pure'.

*   *   *   *   *

Major Cooper: Does the Minister know that it is very hard for farmers to raise the wind?

*   *   *   *   *

Mr Johnson: I think a bull is worth more than a dog.
Mr Hewat: What price a bull dog?

*   *   *   *   *

Professor Magennis: . . . By all means give a fillip to building. . . but if we are to proceed to give subsidies by a remission of rates to those who built some years back on what principle are we to justify that? . . . A man who a few years ago believed that A. B. was the one woman on earth for him selected her to be his wife. Very good. That was a courageous enterprise. After a few years he discovers that he needs a subsidy. He could get a subsidy by removing that wife and taking another who has more money.

*   *   *   *   *

Professor Magennis: I am very much indebted to Deputy McCullough for drawing my attention to what must have been due to my want of clearness. I did not, and I do not intend to, call anyone a bad egg. I did refer to the O.B.E., which is jocosely interpreted to mean, by Englishmen, the Order of the Bad Egg.

*   *   *   *   *

Mr Johnson: . . . I suggest that a reasonable possibility under this section, as it stands at present, would be this: A football team coming home from a country match, marching three or four miles, would, from the very spirit of the thing, be ordered to fall in, and they would march and they would have manoeuvres and the crowd following would join in. An officious policeman comes along and says: 'This is against the Treason and Sedition Act', and he prosecutes these people for performing military manoeuvres. . . .

* * * * *

Mr Johnson: . . . I am reminded of the story of a certain young man who was introduced, from a distance, in the garish lights of a music-hall, to a lady handsome and beautiful, as he thought. He was captivated by her appearance and before he knew where he was –

Mr Baxter: He put his foot in it?

Mr Corish: He was had.

Mr Johnson: He was had, as my friend Deputy Corish says. He took the girl home to be his wife.

Mr Corish: He was all the more had then.

Mr Johnson: And, as one may say, on the Report Stage, he found that his handsome lady was minus a leg, had false teeth –

Mrs Collins O'Driscoll: And glass eyes.

Mr Johnson: Yes, and glass eyes. He found, too, that her beautiful bust had been padded. When all the appurtenances thereof had been removed, he had a different impression. The same applies to this Bill, and one can observe all that has been removed from it as compared with what it contained when introduced. The young man of my story was quite prepared to go before his friends, though he was a modest man, and boast and brag about his lady. I do not know whether he was prepared to boast and brag about her after he had seen her dismantled. Similarly, I do not know whether the Minister is prepared to boast and brag about this Bill now. What Bill is it that he is prepared to boast and brag about? Is it the original Bill, or the new Bill that he is prepared to brag about?

Mr O'Higgins: Both.

Mr Johnson: Yes. Many of the teeth have gone; a wooden leg replaces the original one. Considering that the Minister was prepared to boast and brag about the original Bill, I have no doubt that he looks with sorrow at the decapitated, trunkless, and heartless residue. . . .

*   *   *   *   *

Mr Gorey: Whatever nationalisation means elsewhere, in this country it means inefficiency, waste, going slow, everything undesirable. . .

*   *   *   *   *

Professor O'Sullivan: . . . We might, for that matter, be much happier if we were back in the woods and back to the savage state; but I do not think any of us are fit to go back to that state.
Mr Gorey: The Deputy would cut quite a respectable figure carrying a club.

*   *   *   *   *

Mr J. Daly: I also disagree with this tax on musical instruments. When you put a tax on musical insruments, you put a tax on music. We all know that the Irish are a musical people. Just take the connection between music and education. For instance, take the gramophone in a country house. I hold it is a source of education to the youth of that house. They can listen to John McCormack or they can be talking Scotch to Harry Lauder if they like. They can listen to all the great singers and to all the great orators – that is, if they are not privileged to come here. . . .
(Later)
. . . For instance, if you go to church on Sunday you have beautiful music. You can pray twice as well as a result of that, and with one twist of the organ you fancy you can see the Promised Land. . . .

*   *   *   *   *

Mr Gorey: . . . When you go to pay for fifteen or twenty dogs, or for a pack of hounds, you are furnished with a separate form for each dog, and a separate stamp for each form. The next thing that will be required will be a passport, with the photo of the dog. . . We have too many curs and mongrels in the country. . . .

*   *   *   *   *

Mr Gorey: Very little I know about school-masters and teaching, but when I come to fishing I know a little about it, as I have been at it for ten or fifteen years.

Mr O'Connell: Poaching?

Mr Gorey: I have done both. I can speak with authority on both sides.

Mr Johnson: Is it as a poacher you are speaking now?

*   *   *   *   *

Mr Johnson: . . . there is more damage done by ducks eating the spawn than by fishermen at the mouths of the rivers. . . .

*   *   *   *   *

Major Cooper: . . . Suppose a Spanish army landed near Tralee, as Spaniards have done –

Mr Esmonde: Or a Danish army?

Major Cooper: Or a Danish army, if you wish, has the Chief of the General Staff any set of plans saying that the Limerick Battalion will move out at once to meet the ememy, and the Athlone Battalion will go by train, via Athenry . . . ?

*   *   *   *   *

Mr Burke: . . . Upper Merrion Street, Merrion Square West, and Lower Merrion Street, were constructed on a reinforced concrete foundation and two-inch asphalt. . . .

Major Cooper: Do I understand the Minister to say that Upper Merrion Street was costing more than any other scheme, and that that was due to the anticipated traffic from Cork?

*   *   *   *   *

Mr Gorey: Have you any 'Kruschen Salts feeling' amongst your chargers or artillery horses, or what are you giving them? . . .

(Later)

I am not going to enter into a discussion with regard to advertisments, say of Beecham's pills, on the back of telegram forms. . . .

*   *   *   *   *

Mr Gorey: The Deputy is inclined to be ridiculous. He must have had his dinner.

Major Cooper: Unfortunately the Deputy has had too many amendments to have any dinner at all. . . .

*   *   *   *   *

Major Cooper: . . . I will make the point very briefly. Irish tobacco for the most part is only suitable for blending, if I understand rightly.

Mr Hewat: For blowing your head off.

* * * * *

Major Cooper: . . . I think that the most potent cause and the most potent factor that makes for emigration is the dullness of the country. A village hall, equipped with a wireless set would, for one thing, help a great deal and it would prevent the people in the country from crowding into the towns or going across the Atlantic. . .

* * * * *

Mr Gorey: The Minister referred to culture being available for the farmers. I understand that six months ago it was not available.

Mr Hogan: It can always be had on application to the veterinary branch.

* * * * *

Major Cooper: . . . While men sleep, trees grow very slowly. A man might sleep his lifetime out and he would see a tree grow to no more than a puny height, certainly not to a marketable height.

Mr Wolfe: I have seen trees grow more than that in my time anyhow.

Major Cooper: In Kildare, growth is abnormal.

Mr Davin: Christmas trees.

* * * * *

Mr J. Conlon: . . . I think the mentality of the schoolboy has been much the same all through the ages. We have Shakespeare's line about the school-boy creeping unwillingly to school. I also recall lines that could not have been written by a quiet, docile boy avid for culture and learning. As well as I remember they are as follows:

I wish my master were a hare,
   And all his books hounds were,
And I myself a jolly hunter
   To wind the horn I would not spare.

The following referred to the Civil Service Regulation Bill:

Major Cooper: . . . it is a Bill with two horns, like a dilemma, and I must discuss them in detail, as the Minister did.

Mr Johnson: There is one in the Museum, I think.

*   *   *   *   *

Mr Blythe: . . . If there is no power to discriminate between the sexes when there is cause for it in the Civil Service, then there is no power to discriminate in the Army under the Constitution. There would be no power to prevent a woman going forward for the examination for a military career.

Professor Magennis: The doctor would not pass her.

Mr Blythe: The doctor could not refuse to pass her if the health of the candidate were good.

Professor Magennis: That is the point: her health would not be good, being a woman.

*   *   *   *   *

Mr Beamish: . . . We consider that as we are not yet fully developed we should take two steps instead of one.

*   *   *   *   *

Mr Vaughan: . . . I wonder where will Deputy Johnson, Deputy Magennis, Deputy Baxter and Deputy T. O'Connell go when the fight will start.

A Deputy: To Cork.

*   *   *   *   *

Mr Byrne: One Deputy went back as far as Fionn Mac Cumhaill yesterday.

Mr Gorey: I am sorry he did not stop there.

*   *   *   *   *

Mr D'Alton: . . . Harness that is affected with disease is largely responsible for cases of parasitic mange, glanders, and strangles. . . .

*   *   *   *   *

Sir James Craig: . . . Deputy Cooper knows a great deal about fleas. He did not say anything about other vermin that are more obnoxious than the class of parasite he is more familiar with. . . .

*   *   *   *   *

Mr Wolfe: . . . I think it is worth the Minister's kind consideration. If he would attend any of the fairs throughout the country where so-called second-hand clothing is exhibited, he would see the necessity for this amendment. I say 'so-called second-hand clothing' because I think it is glorifying it to call it 'second-hand'. I think a great deal of it has passed through many more hands than two. I have often wondered that something was not done to regulate this traffic. One sees sometimes a really repulsive garment held out to the admiration of possible purchasers. . . .

*   *   *   *   *

Professor O'Sullivan: . . . Supposing a parent told Katie to tell the teacher that Mary was not able to go to school.
Mr Heffernan: You will have this difficulty; you will compel the illiterate parent to walk to the school to give notice, and that is rather drastic.
Professor O'Sullivan: I am giving him three days to do it.

*   *   *   *   *

Captain Redmond: I hold no brief for the past.
Mr O'Higgins: No. Whereas the judiciary of the past, acccording to Deputy Redmond, were sons of darkness, the judiciary of the future will be all children of the morning, sons of light.
Mr T. O'Connell: Sons of rest.

*   *   *   *   *

Mr Lyons: I suggest that the farmers have spoken and that they do not want to hear anybody else.
Mr Gorey: The restaurant is your place.
Mr Lyons: No, sir. Of course, the coursing field is your place.

*   *   *   *   *

Mr Cole: You cannot sell land down in my place at any price.
The President: Well, bring it up here and sell it here. You will get any price you like for it here.

*   *   *   *   *

Mr Johnson: . . . I think it is a right view to take that the heavy buses and char-a-bancs that are plying for passengers between the cities and the country are too heavy and too fast for the health and safety of the people or the economy of the county councils and the city councils. One has heard for years of the road hog, but we are now faced night by night and day by day with the hippopotamus in the shape of these tremendous instruments of fright that, carrying passengers, cut through the roads travelling at a very fast pace. . . .

*   *   *   *   *

Mr Lyons: I am afraid Deputy Beamish has let the cat out of the bag.
Mr Beamish: It is only a kitten.

*   *   *   *   *

Mr O'Higgins: . . . the Garda outside the Dublin metropolitan area, . . . receives in 1925, two frocks. . . He will receive one great coat in 1926, one in 1930, one in 1934; three in a nine-year period.
Mr Hewat: What would happen if a dog took a piece out of one of them?
Mr O'Higgins: The dog would be shot. . . .

*   *   *   *   *

Mr Sears: . . . Deputy Gorey once seemed to think that it was I put the question as to whether Ireland could not support herself if there was a brass wall round the country.
Mr T. O'Connell: She could sell the brass.

*   *   *   *   *

Major Cooper: Is marriage a matter of discipline?
Mr Johnson: Yes, afterwards.
Mr O'Higgins: Sometimes. . . .

*   *   *   *   *

Mr Connor Hogan: . . . I believe that the flags for a battalion should last for 20 to 25 years. That period does not seem too long.
Mr Johnson: Not with the orange dye we have got.

*   *   *   *   *

Mr O'Connor: . . . I knew a man who had money invested in other business, but he watched the stock and the money markets so closely that his health broke down. He suffered from insomnia. His doctor advised him to give up that business and to put his money into house property. He did so, and invested

£40,000. I built a good deal of property for him. Perhaps he is suffering from insomnia today.

Mr Good: He is dead.

* * * * *

Mr Gorey: I would strenuously object to this class of lunatic being sent down the country.

Sir James Craig: You have them already down there.

Mr Gorey: That may be, but the criminal lunatics are a different class to the ordinary lunatics. . . .

* * * * *

Mr Fitzgerald: I might be permitted to digress and tell a story about a man who was up before a judge. 'Do you always do this?' the judge asked him. 'Yes, my lord, always,' was the reply. 'Remember now, you are speaking on oath,' said the judge. 'Do you always do it?' 'Yes, my lord, almost always,' was the reply. 'Almost always?' asked the judge. 'Yes, my lord, nearly almost always,' replied the man. . . .

* * * * *

Professor O'Sullivan: . . . New York spends from seven to ten times more in comparison with her population on education than we do.

Mr Wilson: Hence the murders.

* * * * *

Professor Magennis: . . . Evidently, in Cork they get their cod from England.

Mr Johnson: And their fluke.

* * * * *

Mr Daly: I hope the day is not far distant when game cocks will be allowed to fight in this country and get a death according to their nature, rather than having the head wrung off them by a cook. . . .

* * * * *

Mr Daly: . . . Stout is one of the necessaries of life.

* * * * *

Major Cooper: Port in this country is regarded as a teetotal drink. If Deputy Daly has never heard of teetotallers in this country drinking port, I do not know whether to congratulate him or to commiserate him. . . .

*   *   *   *   *

Mr Johnson: . . . It would be surprising, I am sure, to Deputies of the male sex if they were to have regard to all the various parts that go to make up a corset.

*   *   *   *   *

Mr Wilson: What is a working-class house?
Mr Johnson: A house occupied by a wage-earner.
Mr Wilson: How many rooms?
Mr Johnson: The question of rooms is a matter of the rate of wages earned by the wage earner.

*   *   *   *   *

Mr Hogan: Does the Minister consider that one o'clock in the morning, on three different occasions, is a desirable hour at which to visit a house?
Mr O'Higgins: It might be the most desirable hour.

*   *   *   *   *

Major Cooper: . . . Rule 16 provides that the person who served the summons shall make a statutory declaration on the back of the original summons, and that such statutory declaration shall be considered sufficient evidence of the service and that it shall not be necessary for the person effecting service to personally attend, which is a split infinitive.
Mr Johnson: That damns it. We cannot approve it.
Major Cooper: I hope that when these are translated into Irish that split infinitive shall be remedied.
Mr O'Connell: You cannot split an Irish infinitive.

*   *   *   *   *

Mr Hogan (Minister): . . . I would ask some Labour Deputy before this debate concludes to quote a sneer or a flippancy used. . . .
Mr Johnson: You cannot put a sneer down on paper.

*   *   *   *   *

Mr Gorey: . . . the law at present is quite a farce when we know the speed at which motor cars can travel with safety on the roads. Deputy Heffernan put the thing in a nutshell when he stated that motorists can travel at twenty, twenty-five or thirty miles a hour. I do not recommend any man to travel faster than thirty miles.

Mr Blythe: Even to a coursing match?

Mr Gorey: In order to go there and come home safely, we would confine ourselves to thirty miles an hour.

Mr Heffernan: Going, but not coming back.

Mr Johnson: . . . there is a very curious provision in the Schedule: 'Loss of one eye, result of G.S.W.' I wonder does that mean loss of one eye due to a Great Swill of Whiskey?

Mr Hughes: No; it is 'gunshot wound'.

* * * * *

Mr J. Conlan: . . . With regard to what is called farmers' butter, or home-made butter, I have it from shopkeepers who are constrained more or less to take this butter in exchange for goods, that they often sell it in Dublin at a loss of 4d. or 5d. per lb. It is practically unsaleable except as car grease. . .

* * * * *

Sir James Craig: . . . He told us that the greater number of priests and nuns in Ireland had their birthplaces in these cross-road public-houses. . . In public-houses frequented by women as well as men, the lavatory accommodation was astounding . . .

* * * * *

Mr Johnson: Would the Minister say what special arrangements are made for looking after the digestive organs of the soldiers when there are no proper cooking arrangements?

* * * * *

Mr Davin: . . . it is a good policy for a person who is in an awkward position to join any organisation that will help him to get out of it. . .

* * * * *

Mr Conlan: Is the minister aware that jurors going to Wicklow from West Wicklow, otherwise than by rail, have to cross a mountain range?

The President: It is easier to do that than to go through it.

* * * * *

Mr Hughes: A man on active service and wearing uniform, whether he was at home or on a day's leave, would clearly come within the section, but if he went away and that something happened to him in the ordinary course, such for instance, as an accident while engaged in kicking football, well he would not come within the section and would not be entitled to a wound pension.

Major Cooper: . . .You may have the case where a man handles his rifle negligently in the barrack room and wounds a man who may be asleep in bed. That man may not be in uniform at all. I do not know if you could say that that man was on duty. . . .

* * * * *

Mr Lyons: . . . In my opinion, closing public-houses on a Saturday night at 9.30 will not mean promoting temperance. I think it will have the contrary effect, because a labouring man obliged to remain at home while his wife is out shopping will not be able to get a drink if he goes out on her return, if the public-houses are closed, or on the point of closing, what he will do is to take a half gallon or a half-dozen of stout to his home and consume it there. I think it would be far better if the public-houses were open until 10 o'clock, and let him consume his drink there rather than in his own home in the presence of his children. The minister is not preventing the capitalist from getting drunk on a Saturday night at 9.30. He can get drink in his club. What I complain of is that workers are prevented from getting a drink on a Saturday night by this 9.30 closing. If the minister ever had to live in a small house he would be aware of all the jobs that the woman of the house has to do on a Saturday night. The husband, as a rule, goes out when she is doing her work, and where is he to go to if he has not the public-house? In most cases the public-house is the drawing-room of the ordinary worker. . .

Professor Magennis: . . . I am afraid the Deputy is over-impressed with the old saying 'drunk as a lord,' so that he conceives drunkenness is a privilege, and that there is class inequality unless facilities are provided for the poor as well as the rich. . .

Mr Lyons: . . . close down clubs such as the Kildare Street Club, and others, not catering for the interests of the working classes.

Professor Magennis: . . . The new reform suggested on behalf of the trade for dealing with those cases of breaches in the licensing laws is that the Guards would take on the functions, fraternal, moral and religious, of exhorting to better ways the man who is already on the point of entering a public-house for the further drink, which ostensibly he could not carry.

* * * * *

Mr McGilligan: . . . the Board, under the terms of this Bill, will be given at any time the power to enter upon the undertaking of any authorised or non-authorised undertaker and take it over on terms set out in the detailed sections. . . .

* * * * *

Mr Gorey: I think that we will have to pass over the pleasantries indulged in by Deputy Morrissey and some other Deputies. I think we may pass over also the speech that was made by Deputy Cooper. It reminded me very much of the Spanish method of making love. Listening to Deputy Cooper one could see in the window 'Miss County Dublin' and outside the Deputy serenading her. . .

* * * * *

Mr Hogan: . . . Take Tipperary with Border Leicesters and Galway ewes – there is no difficulty in keeping them in. In County Galway farmers have gone in for horny ewes and Cheviots and there is no difficulty ever in keeping them in, if you take reasonable precautions. There is no use in the Deputy trying to impress other Deputies, who are not farmers, with that particular difficulty, which does not exist.

Mr Heffernan: The Minister knows that it does exist. There are times of the year when nobody can keep sheep from trespassing – one little gap will let a flock of 40 or 50 go through in a few minutes. The Minister knows it well. You cannot keep cattle in at certain times of the year. I have seen them climb an eight-feet high fence.

Mr Nolan: Would the Minister insert a section that would meet the case of the innocent Tipperary sheep and big red bullocks?

* * * * *

After speaking about plover and bullfinches Mr Wolfe was answered by Major Cooper.

Major Cooper: I am not sure how far Deputy Wolfe was in order in introducing a bull into a discussion on a Bill concerning wild birds. His case is made worse by the fact that the particular bull he introduced was, by some zoological freak, the off-spring of a lion. I am sure every Deputy must have listened with great sympathy to Deputy Wolfe's plea for the caged bird, and must have appreciated his passionate feeling, whenever he saw a bird in a small cage, to liberate it. I only hope the birds will reciprocate that feeling and, if the time ever comes when they will see Deputy Wolfe in a small cage, they will do their best to liberate Deputy Wolfe. . . .

* * * * *

Mr Johnson: The law has had the reputation of being a four-legged animal for a long time, but to find that a society is producing eggs because the members of the society produce eggs comes as a surprise to me.

* * * * *

Mr Daly: . . . In every country in the world our patron saint is going to be honoured except in Ireland where he died and where he sanctified us all, or at least tried to do so. In addition, there are fairs and markets held in some parts of the country on St Patrick's Day. I do not know if the Seanad desire they should be put a stop to. There would be holy war then. . . . I think the Minister should try to convert the Senators the same as St Patrick tried to convert others.

Mr Gorey: . . . It is held, on the other hand, that a slight would be offered St Patrick by having the day wet. . .

2. After Fianna Fáil Take their Seats

On 11 October 1927 Eamon de Valera and his Fianna Fáil Party took their seats in the Dáil for the first time. The action caused a certain amount of controversy and much of the debate which followed reflected this. There were still plenty of light moments, however.

* * * * *

Mr Blythe: . . it might be possible for people, for instance, to detach a crucifix, which is part of a rosary, and to import the crucifix separately and the other parts separately and claim exemption from the duty. It might be possible to separate the rosary into two parts and to say in respect of each, it is not a rosary, and claim exemption from duty. . . .

* * * * *

Major Cooper: . . . that is the great Fianna Fáil cry: 'Down with the maize'. I wonder how the farmers will take that. Then to make up Deputy de Valera's twelve millions there is rice – not a very big import. I suppose they can grow rice in Longford and Westmeath too. . .

* * * * *

The President: Deputy Flinn is an excellent judge of impertinence, judging by his speech this evening. I, unfortunately, am nothing but a child in that matter. . .

* * * * *

Mr O'Kelly: . . The whole of that week's proceedings seemed to me to be a lowering of the dignity that attaches to the municipality of Dublin. We had a week of jazz and a circus of some kind parading the city. Ladies – I do not know anything about them and I do not know anyone who does – were brought here on beauty show. Imagine bringing beauties from outside to a city like Dublin. Someone beside me suggests that it was like bringing coals to Newcastle . . .

* * * * *

Major Cooper: . . . I hope that I shall not offend Deputies who are qualified doctors when I say that their common ancestor was the barber surgeon, who cut your hair, pulled your teeth, and, if required, let blood. . .

* * * * *

Mr Killilea: . . . That reminds me about tales which I hear old women in County Galway telling. They say 'Why are we poor, and why are we in misery?' They ask 'What can we expect from a two-penny halfpenny solicitor?'

* * * * *

Mr Heffernan: . . . As I pointed out earlier, there was a shortage of bags in this country. We met that shortage by the simple, and perhaps not altogether unjustifiable method of retaining the British bags which came across here. We retained the bags. Of course there is a question of reciprocity to a certain extent. Our bags are going to them, but this is for the balance which remains with us. There is always a certain number of bags passing backwards and forwards. . . .

* * * * *

Mr Flinn: . . . .You can get a patent in France and in two or three other countries for the price at which you can apply for a patent in the Free State. You can get a patent for England and for the Free State cheaper than you can get a patent for the Free State alone. That is rather remarkable.

* * * * *

Mr J. J. Byrne: Will the Deputy substantiate that?
Mr Flinn: If that baby would only be good!
Mr Byrne: If the Deputy would only be logical!
Mr Flinn: He is evidently quite impossible. Some day I shall have to spank that baby.
Mr Byrne: That may be more difficult than you anticipate.
Mr Flinn: All right. He has not got a place to be spanked on . . .

* * * * *

Mr Corry: . . . when I look at the list of gentlemen who are drawing Army pensions in East Cork, I find that a lot of them are gentlemen whose only service during the Black-and-Tan trouble was on the few occasions that I had to pull them out of bed, to cut trees.

* * * * *

Mr Jordan: Let the wolves loose again.
Mr J. Wolfe: Let Wolfe after them again. I would rather keep the wolf from the door.
Mr Jordan: So would I.

* * * * *

Mr Carney: . . . these men paid £1,500 for that boat. It was taken away, and nothing left in its place. If you buy furniture from a modern firm on the hire purchase system and if you pay half the price they will allow you to keep half the commodity or give you something.
Mr Blythe: Half a boat.
Mr Carney: Yes but could not a smaller boat have been provided? As a matter of fact, the boat was not much good and half of it would have been much worse. . .

* * * * *

Professor Tierney: . . . the Fianna Fail party in this House has always adopted the attitude of trying to keep a foot in both camps, to keep a foot in the constitutional camp and another foot in the camp which is not constitutional, a camp which is involved in the using of arms against citizens of this country by other citizens of this country, and, if you like, trying to keep a third foot in a third camp.
Mr Aiken: Deputy Tierney took his foot out of one camp in 1916 in any case.
Professor Tierney: I do not know if there is much hope of keeping a foot in the third camp because I think the lady who owns the third camp does not relish the foot being kept there.

* * * * *

Mr Lynch: If you take your hand away from your mouth, Gerry, I could hear what you have to say.
Mr G. Boland: I said you were a good judge of ignorant critics, Finian. I have taken my hand away from my jaw now.
Mr Lynch: Well, put a sock in it.

* * * * *

Mr Corry: . . .Yesterday, my friend, Deputy Cooper – who, after all, I think, has a sense of humour – said that he would rather come here than go to a racecourse; he would get more amusement out of it.

The President: There is a considerable difference between amusement and a joke . . .

Mr Corry: As far as the dignity of the House is concerned, it is, after all, a glorified county council.

Mr Gorey: Perhaps the Deputy is not far out. I see a couple of Deputies amusing themselves with a piece of string, making the place more like a monkey-house.

*　*　*　*　*

Mr Hogan: . . . I will just give a few instances of my experience as a member of the Gaeltacht Commission. I remember dropping into a wayside Civic Guard station. There were two of us. There was an old lady scrubbing the hall, and as she was rather in my way I said, 'Bail a Dhia ort. Cad atá tu ag deanamh annso?' or something like that. Oh, said she, 'Beannacht leat.' I am not quite sure yet whether it was a polite invitation to me to get out, whether she was handing me my hat and coat, or whether she was actually speaking the couple of words of Irish she knew. And this was in the Gaeltacht. I went inside and I said a few words of Irish to a constable. He looked me up and down. He did not know Irish. I am not saying this now as a joke against the Civic Guards. There are Irish speakers in the Civic Guard and I do not intend to make any point against them, but I am endeavouring to point out what will happen if there is not more close contact with whoever is put in charge of this mission to the Gaeltacht, because it is a mission. The constable looked at me in surprise. I asked him something else in Irish and he said to me, 'What do you want?' He emphasised 'Want!' I said. 'I want an Irish-speaking Civic Guard.' He said, 'You had better go in to the sergeant.' I went in to the sergeant, and he was discoursing a beef-steak inside. I spoke to him in Irish. He said, 'What do you want?'

A Deputy: Poteen.

Mr Hogan: No, I did not want poteen. But this was in the Gaeltacht. I said, 'If I continued speaking Irish to you, what would you do?' He said, 'I would eject you from the room.'

*　*　*　*　*

Mr A. Byrne: There are three members on the Fianna Fáil side
of the House asleep, and three on the other.

An Ceann Comhairle: The position is that when a Deputy's eyes
are shut the Deputy is not necessarily asleep.

Mr MacEntee: Could we test that?

*   *   *   *   *

Mr Little: Today is really tomorrow.

*   *   *   *   *

Mr J. Wolfe: . . . Has the Evil Literature Bill anything to do with
the reporting of the proceedings in the Dáil?

*   *   *   *   *

Mr Mac Entee: . . . Deputy Tierney, the Deputy who has no
head for politics, is the blushing parent of this new Constitutional
proposal. He did not attempt indeed to justify or defend this
progeny of his, which, like a political Vulcan, has sprung from
the brain of the Zeus who has no head for politics.

Professor Tierney: On a point of explanation. I do not think that
Vulcan sprang from anybody's brain.

Mr J. Wolfe: His thunder did not fall from heaven.

Professor Tierney: He fell from Heaven.

Mr Mac Entee: Anyway, apparently, the Deputy is a greater
authority upon mythology than upon politics. . .

*   *   *   *   *

Mr Mac Entee: . . . When we see the President now come into
this House and asking the House now to delete these Articles
from the Constitution, it reminds me of a few lines I once heard
and which I remember:

'You are old, Father William,' the young man said,
   'And your hair has become very white,
And yet you incessantly stand on your head,
   Do you think at your age it is right?'

'In my youth,' Father William replied to the son,
   'I feared it might injure the brain,
But now that I am perfectly sure I have none,
   Why, I do it again and again.'

*   *   *   *   *

Mr Anthony: . . . I hope that Deputies discussing this Bill will separate the City Manager from the existing City Commissioner. . . . it would be far better to continue the present system of City Commissionership than to set up what to me would appear to be a sort of 'Pooh-Bah' for the City of Cork. . . If the people pay the piper, they should call the tune? If the Cork people ask for 'The Top of Cork Road', and the Manager says, 'they will have a Beethoven Sonata', where are we?

* * * * *

Mr Fitzgerald-Kenney: . . . Deputy Brady said that there were persons there who were very disorderly. He also said that there were women whose reputation – I might put it this way – is very shady who frequent Clondalkin. I think that is highly probable, but they cannot be arrested, or they cannot be dealt with by the police, no matter what their reputation may be or no matter what conclusion you may draw from their appearance as to their profession. The Guards cannot deal with these women. They cannot arrest them unless they become drunk . .
Mr Brady: I referred to a particular case where a man was not able to stand.

* * * * *

Mr Mac Entee: . . . let the Parliamentary Secretary to the Minister for Finance, the very able chief Whip of the Government Party, for once enact the role of 'Little Bo-Peep.' Let him bring home his sheep and let them bring their votes behind them. . .

* * * * *

Mr Law: . . . Let us take, for example, four books and apply the test to them. I cannot imagine how they would be dealt with. I will take two English and two French. Take a story like *Boule de Suif,* by de Maupassant; take that remarkable play, *Les Trois Filles* de M. Dupont, not books *pour les jeunes personnes;* take the play *Mrs Warren's Profession,* by Bernard Shaw, or take, finally, the last book of the same author *The Intelligent Woman's Guide to Capitalism and Socialism.* Three of these works that I have mentioned deal not merely incidentally but I suppose *ex professo,* at any rate have as their subject matter, very scandalous and delicate subjects – prostitution and venereal disease. The third deals, at least incidentally in a passage or two at any rate, with these matters. . . .

*   *   *   *   *

Sir James Craig: . . . It is an extraordinary thing that I found when a book had been mentioned four or five members of the Dáil rushed to get hold of it because it had been put on the prohibited list. . . .

*   *   *   *   *

Professor Alton: . . . Savage nations, you know, have periodical orgies of smelling out witchcraft, which they enjoy very much. Those are organised. Here the Minister is organising and recognising – well, the word 'informers' is an obnoxious word and I will not use it for the gentleman who will fill the office, but he is organising delatores, and is going to stimulate numerous groups of them. I can see those associations, worked up to a white heat by friendly rivalry and puritan zeal, sending in denunciations to the Minister by every post. . . .

*   *   *   *   *

Domhnall Ua Buachalla:. . . . A short time ago I had occasion to visit a poor woman in an out-of-the -way place in County Meath, about three miles from Maynooth. This woman lived in a two-roomed thatched cabin, and a storm took away half the roof one night. She asked me to go out to have a look at it to see if I could do anything for her. This poor woman and I were sitting by the fire in the kitchen – the roof had been taken off the bedroom. . . I saw on a shelf inside the chimney breast a box with some books in it. 'Biddy,' said I to the woman. 'I see you have some books here. Perhaps there may be some valuable old Irish manuscripts among them. May I have a look at them?' She said that I might. I took down the box and examined the contents. There were about ten copies of the *Irish Rosary* and just as many copies of these filthy novels, novels with attractively coloured covers, with their suggestive, immoral, filthy stories. . .

*   *   *   *   *

Mr Boland: . . . I saw the official shouting across the House.
Mr Fitzgerald-Kenney: The Deputy saw a shout!

*   *   *   *   *

Mr Fitzgerald-Kenney: . . . If you put in 'corrupt or deprave in sexual matters' I do not think it would be wide enough. . . It could be done in this way, by using words 'likely to suggest or incite to sexual immorality or unnatural vice or in any other similar way'. That is putting 'similar' instead of 'like' which is synonymous, in order to get the hang of the thing. . . .

* * * * *

An amendment (18) to read that 'All meetings of the (Censorship) Board should be held in public' gave rise to the following remark.
Mr Fitzgerald Kenney: . . . I am afraid those public debates would be attended by all the prurient-minded persons in Dublin, and that there would be a great deal of reading of immoral passages for their delection.

* * * * *

Dr Ryan: I do not want to divide the House on dirty eggs.

* * * * *

Mr Broderick: I do not think the medical officer of health is operating in Co Westmeath.

* * * * *

Mr Derrig: . . . Deputy Moore asked the Minister how could it be determined that the offals were from the previous day.
Mr Lynch: They will speak for themselves.

* * * * *

The President: . . . The leader of the Opposition, who in absentia was nominated as President of the Executive Council last year, was absent from this House from December of last year until June of this year. These are the people who say to us 'five months' holiday'. What was he doing outside of this country when the Budget of this State was being discussed here?
Mr Gorey: Robbing the servant girls of America.

* * * * *

In reply to a question as to whether fees of factory directors had decreased, Mr Gorey replied

Mr Gorey: If the Deputy is referring to me, I can tell him that my fee is half-a-crown a day and third class rail fare. My fee has not come down. . . When I go to Waterford I get a half-a-crown for lunch – a good lunch – and third class rail fare.

*   *   *   *   *

Mr Cassidy: I should like to ask the Minister if any of these worn out horses which have been exported from this country have been sold in shops in Dublin as tinned beef. . . .

Mr Kent: How many of these worn out horses are in use in foreign cavalry regiments?

Mr McGilligan: I do not know what a worn out horse is.

*   *   *   *   *

Mr Little did not go along with drinking intoxicating liquor on the National Apostle's feastday.

Mr Little: In gazing down upon the Minister when he was introducing this Bill, I could not help thinking of the famous sonnet of Shelley, which began: ' I met a traveller from an antique land who said he could not get a drink on Patrick's Day.' The Minister seems to be, in my mind, that traveller from the antique land. He is like Rip Van Winkle. He has apparently been unaware of the place in the course of the national struggle which the question of not drinking on Patrick's Day has always taken. . . I regret to say Irishmen do get drunk on St Patrick's Day. . . The Scottish, I regret to say have a way of honouring St Andrew's Day in somewhat in a similar manner. . . do you think that we would not admire them if they succeeded in the movement in Scotland in abstaining from drink on St Andrew's Day. . . (do) you think anyone would consider that a slur on the Scottish people?

Mr Anthony: It is easy to abstain from Scotch Whiskey.

3. Fianna Fáil in Power

The first Fianna Fáil Government came into power on 9 March 1932.

Mr McGilligan: . . . It now appears that the Minister for Finance is starring tomorrow at the Gaiety Theatre. Is the President prepared to put down the estimate for tomorrow and recall the Minister for Finance from the Gaiety Theatre?

(Later)

. . . If it is found that if the Minister will be occupied at the Gaiety Theatre tomorrow, he will be recalled in order to attend the important business of the Drumm Battery. . . .

* * * * *

Mr Cosgrave: . . . I would have the temperament of Deputy Davin if I took to drinking tea. He is timorous, supercilious and provocative. I am none of these things.

Mr Davin: You are a good advertisement for Oxo.

* * * * *

Mr MacDermot: . . . Why not go to them (the British Government) and say: 'Look here, we will never have any health in Ireland as long as the Treaty is made the foundation of our constitution. . . .'

* * * * *

Mr McGilligan: . . . Where is the Bill?

Mr S. Jordan: In cold storage.

Mr McGilligan: Like the back benchers of Fianna Fáil.

General Mulcahy: It is in the dissecting room.

* * * * *

An Ceann Comhairle: Discussion of the Butter Bill is definitely out of order on this motion.

Mr Cleary: He will bring in the Drumm train yet.

Mr McGilligan: If the Butter Bill had been brought here on it, it would have come a great deal faster.

Mr O'Kelly: How many times in the last month was the Drumm train brought in for repairs?

Mr McGilligan: I would remind the Vice-President that, like a human organism, a battery can go out of order occasionally.

* * * * *

Mr Bennett: . . . We are rapidly getting nearer to nature. I fear that in a very short time it is only the very rich who will be able to afford anything in the line of boots or clothing, except something perhaps in the form of a bathing costume.

Mr Anthony: Or a fig leaf.

* * * * *

Mr O'Neill: . . . If you abolish Guinness's stout what are you going to substitute for it in the City of Dublin?

A Deputy: Beamish's.

Mr O'Neill: No. 'Spanish Ale will give you hope, my dark Rosaleen.' Take care that Spanish ale may have a lot of froth on it, and it may contain some corrosive acid that will eat into the vitals of our country.

* * * * *

Mr MacEntee: . . . nothing will get under the Deputy's skin.

Mr Morrissey: Except a white elephant.

* * * * *

Mr McGilligan: . . . Are there handles of brushes and brooms that are not made of wood?

Mr Lemass: Toothbrushes.

* * * * *

Mr McGilligan: The Minister should not interrupt so much. It has been said that when you go sailing the Spanish Main, and garbing yourself in the reddest of sashes, carrying the blackest of flags and arming yourself with the hugest of cutlasses, you should not also have the tenderest of skin.

* * * * *

Mr McGilligan: The talk about business and the preparation for business comes badly from a Government which has introduced the system of sleeping over its work. Until the present Government made its appearance, there were no such things as beds in Government Buildings while work was being done. It takes people now to sleep at their work.

Parliamentary Secretary to the President (Mr G. Boland): The Deputy can bring his bed here tonight.

Mr McGilligan: There is an ancient joke about a man who appeared at the office one day and explained his absence by saying that he overslept himself at home, and his employer said: 'Good God! Do you sleep there too?' The Ministry apparently have the same habits. They sleep away from their work and they have beds at their work.

* * * * *

Mr Anthony: Some of us think that there should be a distinction drawn between dances and ordinary athletic pursuits.

* * * * *

Mr McGilligan: Ottawa is not a foreign game.

* * * * *

Mr Bennett: . . . I am reminded of a very old story. A bull was once bitten by a warble fly. To escape the pain the bull ran away, as bulls do. The nearest object to him was a hay rick, and in the endeavour to brush off the fly he proceeded to run and run around the hay rick until at last he overtook himself, and pucked himself out of the way. I hope the day is not so far distant when the present Ministry will succeed in getting themselves out of the way in the same manner as the bull did.

* * * * *

General Mulcahy: We are simply dealing then with balls and dances not sports?

Mr MacEntee: Sports and dances, and even the Dáil as a place of entertainment, were discussed by Deputy McGilligan. . . .

Mr Dillon: I take it the Minister is not serious when he says that if I take part in the 'Waves of Tory' I pay no tax, but if I take part in a foxtrot I do pay tax?

Mr M. Hayes: If you take part in the 'Waves of Tory' and speak in English you are not, but if you take part in a fox-trot and speak in Irish you are. I have done both.

* * * * *

Mr O'Neill: You, sir, were not in the Chair on the last night when we were discussing amendments 54 to 59, dealing with dances and football. What are we discussing at present?

Mr Jordan: You are in a scrum now.

* * * * *

Mr Gorey: . . . I consider that a tax on sport is a tax on health and physical development. I think that this is a tax on fresh air and national health. . . When one contrasts the period about 1922, when I came to Dublin – I had been, of course, in Dublin in connection with Gaelic matters before – in 1932, one is struck by the improvement in the appearance and physique of the young ladies of the city. That is apparent to anybody coming up from the country, while it may not be so apparent to those living here permanently. I have heard everybody comment on it – the robust health, the physique, and the excellent physical development of the young ladies of the city. . . .

* * * * *

Mr Gorey: I have not much sympathy either with the man who speaks about a particular way in which you hit the football. I do not see how these things make any difference at all. In the old days the insides of the ball were not made of rubber. The inside was got from the local butcher or from the local horse-knacker. I remember the time when we got rubber insides first.

* * * * *

Mr Dockrell: . . . I should like to ask the Minister does he wish to tax galavanised steel riveted tanks, cisterns and cylinders?

Mr Lemass: Yes.

Mr Dockrell: Who is going to make them?

Mr Lemass: There is a firm which specialises in the manufacture of these.

Mr Dockrell: Would the Minister mind giving the name?

Mr Lemass: Messrs Held.

Mr Dockrell: They certainly galvanise.

* * * * *

Mr Dockrell: . . . I would much rather that the Minister was up on the 60-foot extension ladder, made by a saw miller who has had no experience, then that I was up on it. . . .

(Later)

Mr Hayes: . . . It must be remembered that the people who have to go up on them are generally trade unionists, with a strong trade union behind them, and they will not go up.

* * * * *

Mrs Collins-O'Driscoll: . . . A live hare in the opinion of a great many people would include an electric hare. . . .

* * * * *

Mr Aiken: . . . Where is this Irish Opposition we were to have? We have had nothing here, for the past couple of months, but a pro-British Opposition.
Mr Hogan: Bunkum, cant!
Mr Aiken: And it is not going to work.
Mr Hogan: That stunt will not work, either. That cock will not fight.

* * * * *

Mr Gorey: . . . This is not a babies' debating society.
Mr MacEntee: It sounds like it.

* * * * *

Mr M. O'Reilly: There was a trade developed with France a few years ago, as Deputy Hogan well knows.
Mr Hogan (Galway): For strippers, say.

* * * * *

Dr Ryan: We all know that wheat must be millable. The miller will mill it and, if he mills it, it is millable. . . .

* * * * *

Mr McGilligan: Just another question. I see a cryptic explanation in Number 10: 'In the Second Column at this reference number the word "vegetables" shall be construed as including tomatoes and cucumbers and cognate words shall be construed accordingly.' Would the Minister point out a 'cognate word' that has been construed accordingly?
Mr Lemass: Vegetable soup.

* * * * *

Mr Dillon: . . . The items mentioned in this long list are in fact excluded from the Schedule for which a permit is required.

Professor O'Sullivan: They are excluded from the exclusions.

Mr Corry: I regret I cannot quote the Deputy's speech. I suppose it must be like the dream he had of the kicking cow – it has vanished with the years.

Mr Fitzgerald-Kenney: It was the Deputy who was dreaming of the kicking cow.

Mr Corry: If you gave that cow a good feed on Indian meal now, it would kick better.

*   *   *   *   *

Mr Lemass: . . . I said the practice of steering a ship with a tiller is obsolete.

Mr O'Neill: Not at all. I steered a boat not very long ago and I know what I am talking about. I would like to ask the Minister if he has any definition for the words 'hard over'? If you are steering a ship you would say to the helmsman 'hard over'. I was discussing this question with some Deputies this evening and I said I did not know what 'hard over' would mean under the present Government, but that I knew what 'hard-up' meant under the present Government.

*   *   *   *   *

Mr Moore: . . . I met a man in Dublin last week, a constituent of mine, who owns a lorry. He brought up a load of potatoes for a neighbour and he was going to bring back groceries and other things to sell in his shop. When the Bill is passed he will not be allowed to carry that load to Dublin.

General Mulcahy: Why not?

Mr Moore: Not for his neighbour. The load I mentioned was for a neighbour and was done for hire.

Mr Davin: He did it for love.

*   *   *   *   *

Mr Flinn: . . . When Irish beef looks beautifully red and the fat looks beautifully white and if you were a cannibal you would go and eat it right away, it is not fit for eating. . . There was a time when they used to take that stuff from out under the counter or from the back of the shop. Now they hang it up because it will stand hanging up. . . Blood is thicker than water and some heads are thicker than blood. (Interruption.) Some are so thick that their mouths cannot stay quiet.

Mr Belton: Even Parliamentary Secretaries' heads.

Mr Flinn: That is solid from there to there. Blood is thicker than water, and because we have quarrelled with the benevolence of John Bull in a single and sacred market –

Mr Keating: Are you not one of John Bull's calves?

Mr Flinn: I am one of John Bull's cows, almost an elephant – a whole zoo. . . .

* * * * *

Mr Anthony: . . . I deprecate extremely the bad taste, to give it a very mild term, of Deputies on the opposite benches when they are allowed to refer to a member of another House in another country as 'Jimmy Thomas'. Now I wonder would our national pride be outraged, would that fighting spirit in our race be outraged, if we heard our Minister for Finance referred to in the British House of Commons as 'Johnny MacEntee'.

* * * * *

Mr MacEntee: The trouble about Deputy Belton is that he is a financial astronomer –

* * * * *

Mr O'Neill: . . . a lorry driver might engage in conversation with a man, whom he would then take for a lift. The result is that the driver of the vehicle does not properly mind his job. He will probably stop at the nearest public-house and the two of them will have a drink. That occurs several times in the course of the journey until finally, the passenger reaches his destination. . . If the person taken up happens to be a lady – and girls are frequently taken up in these lorries by the drivers – there is a serious temptation to waste the driver's time. . . There were two cases where such parties went to the Cork Fair one evening; they were late going home. . . .

* * * * *

Mr Bennett . . . Everybody knows that cattle coming towards you provide by their eyes the greatest reflector that can be produced. Anybody who on a dark night could not see the eyes of a flock of sheep or cattle coming towards him does not deserve to be allowed to drive a motor car. . . .

* * * * *

Mr T. Kelly: . . . The cult of the picture house and the cult of the jazz shop is, I think, affecting very considerably and in a not very pleasant way – I want to be very careful of the words I use, as I am generally not too careful – the disposition of our people. I know myself, personally, that in this city a large number of men and women have been thrown out of employment by the mechanisation of the picture shop. I have never seen a 'talkie'. I do not know what it is like. I never propose to see one; but I understand from those who are habitual picture-goers that there is really a very big change, from the point of view of culture, between the silent pictures and the present 'talkies'. People tell me that it used to be a pleasure, from a musical standpoint, to go into those picture-houses years ago, and that this is all changed now. I suppose that the general wish for this unhealthy excitement and love-stuff that is being circulated now in every picture house throughout this country has demoralised, in some way at any rate, the better sense of our people. . . .

*   *   *   *   *

Mr J. M. Burke: . . . I have no doubt that some Ministers, in the course of their duties, see fields now and again on the ordnance map, but honestly, I would not entrust them with the management of Mrs Wigg's cabbage patch. . . They neither sow nor reap nor gather into barns, but they lay down rules and regulations with an assurance that would put Liebeg, Baldwin and Wibberly into the halfpenny place. . . I am very sorry that the House is tonight without the stately presence of Deputy Hugo Flinn. On the last occasion he solemnly told Deputy Fitzgerald-Kenney that he was elected not as a prophet, but as a Deputy. . . In the course of his speech he used on several occasions the phrase, 'A nation's ransom'. Oh, the blessed word 'Mesopotamia'. He evidently has a copyright of that expression. More than once I heard him use it in Cork. It is evidently clinging on to him. It is like asthma. He tries to get it off his chest, but he cannot. As he is not here, I shall part with him with this remark:

> In all his humours, whether grave or mellow,
> He is such a touchy, testy clever fellow;
> There's so much skill and so much spleen about him,
> There is no living with him or without him.

I should like to add by way of prayer, 'May perpetual lime-light shine upon him. . . .'

* * * * *

Mr Kelly: . . . Last Friday when I left this House to open my shop at 2 o'clock in the day, a well-dressed elderly woman came and said to me: 'Could you tell me the name of Steve Donoghue's mount in today's race?' She was no more a sportswoman than I am a woman. I gave her the name of Steve Donoghue's mount in the day's race and I asked her would I put paper and cord around it so that she would not lose it on the way home. She grew very indignant and left my shop very angry at the idea of being received in such a discourteous manner. If any of you here want Steve Donoghue's mount, or Canty's mount, or Beary's mount, or Gordon Richard's mount or any other mount will you consult me by appointment. . . .

(Later)

. . . There is another correspondent of the same name of Kelly from South Africa who sends me enclosures for Sweepstakes. He, I think, described himself in one of his letters as 'agent', 'trader' or 'commercial traveller'. Evidently he was inducing the natives in that portion of the world to buy Sweepstake tickets, because he told me in his second letter that I would not believe the interest the people there were taking in Dublin now. That took a good deal of worry off me because I was always anxious that the natives of South Africa would think well of Dublin.

* * * * *

Mr Cosgrave: The Minister is going mad. We will divide on that question.

* * * * *

Mr Dillon: Might I remind the Minister that vitamins are also more fully present in cod liver oil? I do not know whether he would like to take cod liver oil with his tea or that people would like to use oat husks. I suggest that the Minister should pour cod liver oil over his porridge.

* * * * *

Mr Good: Good women would be better than bad men.

* * * * *

Mr T. Kelly: I wish it were half-past ten.

Mr Dillon: I can quite understand that Deputy Kelly is not profoundly interested in the pig industry. He has no reason to be. He would not know one end of a pig from the other if he saw it. . . I do not bemoan his eloquence. I expect a similar courtesy from him.

Mr Kelly: I am not bemoaning your eloquence at all. I am only wishing it were half-past ten.

(Later)

Mr Dillon: It is an interesting thing to notice that whenever we proceed to get down to the real results of the Fianna Fáil policy on the interests of the farming community in this country, the stock jokers of the Fianna Fáil Party are summoned in from the Lobby, one after another. The feeble jesters of the patriotic Party, the buffoons of the Party of integrity in Ireland, are produced for the purpose of raising a laugh. . . One of the great virtues of a buffoon is that he has a hide like a rhinoceros. The more you display his imbecility the more imbecile he delights in becoming. . . .

Mr Bennett: Traitors to the pigs!

(Later)

Mr Dillon: . . . Sub-paragraph (d), however, is the jewel of this motion. It is really delicious – 'To regulate hygienically the conditions under which pig husbandry is carried on.' One can picture the drawing-rooms and the boudoirs and the beauty parlours that will be provided for the pigs.

Mr Belton: And the Turkish baths.

Mr Dillon: One can picture the Minister's anxiety lest the pigs go to market with their hands unwashed and one can picture his despair because the curl in some particular pig's tail has not the spring and the coils it should have.

Mr Jordan: And the permanent wave.

*   *   *   *   *

Mr Anthony: . . . I know I am going to bring down a lot of trouble on myself from the various temperance organisations. I am not indulging in vote-catching. I do not suppose I got one vote from a publican in the City of Cork. . . It would be far better if drink were made cheaper. . . If that were done in Donegal and whatever constituency Deputy Smith represents, there would not be so much poteen consumed and the lunatic asylums would not be as full as they are.

*   *   *   *   *

Mr Anthony: . . . I can sit down on that note having given the house an illustration of the state to which agriculture is being reduced when an old settle inside a half-door is considered to be more valuable than a full-grown heifer.

Mr O'Leary: In Macroom a farmer told me some time ago that he sold a cow for a bob, but the buyer was so conscientious that he gave him two shillings. . . .

* * * * *

Mr Corry: . . . Nothing is any good to the rancher I admit. There is no good in giving him a butter bounty when he keeps no cow.

Mr Fagan: We want a free market.

Mr Corry: That is the trouble. If he could get the bullock to milk it would be all right.

Mr Fagan: We have more than bullocks in our constituency.

Mr Corry: We are prepared to give the farmer who follows the plough all the assistance we can.

Mr Belton: That farmer only wants fair play.

Mr Corry: You do not know anything about him.

Mr Belton: I forgot more than ever you learned or any members of your party.

* * * * *

Mr Fagan: On a point of order. Deputy Corry referred to me as a bullock.

Mr Corry: No

An Leas-Cheann Comhairle: What is the point of order?

Mr Dillon: The point of order is that disgusting scurrility should not be allowed. . .

Minister for Agriculture (Dr Ryan): I think the time has come when Deputies opposite should allow Deputy Corry to make his speech.

Mr Dillon: If that is the nature of his speech it would be much better not made.

Dr Ryan: Let him finish his speech. . .

Mr Corry: I should like Deputy Fagan to understand that I did not make the statement which he attributes to me. I would not make it in this House. I said that the particular class of farmers, namely, bullock ranchers, would gain nothing by the butter subsidy because their bullocks would not milk.

Mr Fagan: You looked very hard at me. . .

* * * * *

Mr O'Kelly: . . . What is the meaning of the word 'politics'?

Mr T. Kelly: The science of government.

Mr O'Kelly: And if we want to govern here, a municipality or a country, we will have to know a good deal about politics and have many political discussions.

Mr Davin: Butter politics.

Mr Corry: The people to whom you have paid pensions here for the last seven years, gentlemen who pulled girls out of their beds in Kerry and whipped them around the road. . . .

*   *   *   *   *

Mr Corry: The Deputy has the wrong job. He ought to be bolting musk-rats in Nenagh; he would make a good ferret.

*   *   *   *   *

An Leas-Cheann Comhairle: Deputies of this Dáil must not be referred to as jackasses.

*   *   *   *   *

Mr McGilligan: What happens to the wives of civil servants when they reach the higher paid ranks? Are they all murdered?

Mr Derrig: I do not know, but it might be a subject of profitable investigation.

*   *   *   *   *

Professor Alton: . . . I would ask the Minister seriously to consider whether that clinging so fiercely to every word and line in the Bill is not a little suspicious. It is rather like the way in which the gentleman of rather easy habits will cling to the lamp post. He does not support the lamp post, but he thinks it may disguise his own instability. I think the Minister is unstable, and I should like him to discuss the matter on its own merits, away from the terms of the Bill.

Mr McEntee: A person in the unstable position pictured by the metaphor would not be able to discuss anything on its merits. He would probably take a very rosy view of his own argument.

Mr McGilligan: That is very like the Minister.

Mr McEntee: Precisely.

*   *   *   *   *

Professor Alton: I should like to know does the term 'currants' cover what the grocer ordinarily means by that term?

Dr Ryan: No, it only applies to fresh currants.

Professor Alton: Should not that be expressed in the Bill? The customs officers are very nice people, I know, but if you give them an inch they are inclined to take an ell.

Mr Dillon: I should like to say a word in defence of the humble prune.

Dr Ryan: Only fresh prunes are intended, of course.

Mr Dillon: That is a new one on me. I have never met a fresh prune. Has anybody in the House ever met a fresh prune? I understood that it was a dried commodity.

Dr Ryan: Possibly, but we do not know what may be grown in this country yet.

Mr Dillon: I should think that a fresh prune would be beyond the persuasive powers even of President de Valera.

* * * * *

Mr Dillon: Does the reference here mean a stretcher to carry a prostrate corpse or a stretcher to make shoes fit?

Mr Lemass: Both.

* * * * *

Mr Aiken: Deputy Dillon is so stupid in all his declarations here that the more he thinks of me the less I think of myself.

Mr Dillon: Deputy Dillon will raise a blister on you.

Mr Aiken: Yes, when everything is peaceful he will raise blisters. Very little blisters he raised when blisters were being raised.

* * * * *

Mr Coburn: He boasts of shooting men from behind a ditch.

Mr Killilea: How did Deputy Coburn shoot them?

Mr Aiken: Deputy Coburn should not be talking at all.

Mr Coburn: I can talk to you inside or outside this House and you cannot prevent me from talking here or anywhere in Ireland. I never carried a rifle or a revolver but I have a pair of hands and I am prepared to use them against any one of you.

Mr Aiken: Deputy Coburn never carried a rifle or revolver but he advised other people to carry them.

Mr Coburn: I never did.

Mr Corry: You did.

Mr Coburn: I never fired at any man in the dark.

* * * * *

Mr Lynch: You will find plenty of them in the Civil Service.
Mr Corry: Those temporary-permanent officials.

* * * * *

Mr Hogan: I say a perfectly fresh egg could be a trade egg.
(Later)
Mr Dillon: But the type of trade egg that causes most difficulty is the stale egg.
Mr Bennett: The election egg.

* * * * *

Mr Belton: . . . I asked the Minister to mention one strain of wheat grown in the country that will produce a flour sufficiently rich in gluten to give us a good bakers' bread. The Minister has not mentioned one. I can make the positive statement, without fear of contradiction, that there is not one that is economic.
Mr Donnelly: What about Arthur Griffith!
Mr Belton: Arthur Griffith is not a wheat.

* * * * *

Mr Morrissey: . . . I think it was admitted and it was recognised by most people that as a result of the passing of this bill and the setting up of a factory or factories in this country, cement would be increased in price by at least 50 per cent. over and above what it is today. The Minister, I notice, smiles at that.
Mr T. Crowley: A concrete smile.
Mr Morrissey: There is one thing about the Minister, unlike some of his colleagues, his smile is not a fixed smile. He has, if I may say so with all respect, a sense of humour. It is a great pity some of his colleagues have not got it.
Mr Crowley: Cement wash.

* * * * *

Mr Lemass: I cannot quite follow Deputy Dillon. When he was speaking, he reminded me of one of those circus turns where a man comes out and wrestles with himself. Deputy Dillon wrestled with himself for five minutes and then knocked himself out. . . .

* * * * *

Mr McGilligan: . . . I am able to say that the statement was made by Deputy Cooney in Grangegorman, not at it. May I say that

that is an appropriate spot for most of the Fianna Fáil promises
to be made in.

Mr MacEntee: Will the Deputy leave Grangegorman and come
to the Dail?

* * * * *

Mr Kelly: . . . The idea of advertising Dublin at that time three
years ago by Civic Week, with gondolas on the Liffey and King
Brian Boru's bird cage on O'Connell Bridge, was all eye-wash,
because the main concern of the Dublin citizens was to secure
decent houses for the inhabitants of Dublin.

* * * * *

Mr O'Grady: I have frequently heard of young men of 50
referred to as boys, and this is often the case in rural parts of
the country.

Mr Dillon: And young ladies of 50 as little girls.

* * * * *

Mr Hales: Will you give us any help in building up that market
instead of criticising us.

Mr Belton: Why did you not ask for it in time before you got
into the soup?

Mr Kehoe: There are more than Deputy Hales in the soup.

Mr O'Leary: There are and they are deeper in the soup than he is.

Mr Kehoe: There is more than soup on the horizon; there is
skilly, I believe.

* * * * *

Mr T. Kelly: . . . Nobody that I ever could trace in my ancestry
was a farmer – certainly on the paternal side anyway. I went
back a long way at one time to find out something about my
family history in the City of Dublin. I went back well over one
hundred years, but I had to stop because there was a woman
amongst my ancestors who was not as good as she might be. I
had to stop then or goodness knows what else I might discover. . .
I am not an agriculturist and, in order that I might learn
something about the consequences to this country, I ask the
ordinary man and woman in the street who I know would not
be liars, their opinions on this matter. I put questions to them
regarding the position of affairs in the country. I can give you
a lot of instances of what their replies were. One was a

professional man, who is an architect and was a strong Unionist.
I remember when, if he could not sing 'Rule Britannia', he used
to whistle it. I asked him how things were and he put his hand
gently on my shoulder and said: 'The best Government we ever
had.' The next man I asked was a County Dublin farmer, whose
family has been in business for generations. When I asked him
how are things, he said: 'Very good.' I am only speaking of
people as I find them. A lady came into my shop some time ago
on a certain business, she said to me: 'I came all the way from
Kildare to see you and I am only just after arriving.' I asked her:
'What were you doing in Kildare?' She said: 'I am travelling; I
travel amongst the small farmers of the country.'

Mr Rogers: Who ever saw a lady travelling amongst small
farmers?

Mr T. Kelly: . . . The next man I met was a commercial traveller
in millinery, and I said to myself: 'Now this man surely must be
down and out.' I asked him how was he getting along and he
said: 'I am doing remarkably well. Since the week before St
Patrick's Day, we have been working overtime.' I asked: 'Is it
selling hats you are?' 'Yes,' he said, 'it is selling hats and I never
had a better time.' I asked him was it to the farmers' wives and
daughters he was selling hats and he said: 'Yes, they have got
the latest fashions, and what is more they look remarkably well
in them.

*   *   *   *   *

Mr Jordan: I was calling the Minister's attention to your remark
that men sitting on these benches are standing.

*   *   *   *   *

Mr Fitzgerald-Kenney: . . . in the County Tipperary there used
to be a football game in which one parish played against another
parish and the ball was brought to its destination by using any
method the players liked – either by kicking it or boxing it with
their hands or catching it and running with it. A boy who had
played this game in Tipperary was afterwards sent to Rugby
College, and while being educated there he went out to play
the ordinary game of football, which was, I think, something on
the lines of Association football – that it is a foul if the ball
touches your hand and so on – but this boy became intensely
excited and, forgetting that he was in Warwickshire and not in
Tipperary, he caught up the ball and ran away with it as hard

as he could. That gave the players and the authorities of Rugby School a different idea, and so the game now known as Rugby was founded. The old principle that you could either kick the ball or run with the ball was introduced by this boy from Tipperary to English football for the first time.

Therefore, Rugby is a foreign game so far as England is concerned, but nobody in England starts up to declare that it is wrong to play it because it is foreign. . . .

* * * * *

Mr Belton: You were cocky when I brought you in here.
Dr Ryan: You?
Mr Belton: Yes. You were singing songs of Caithlin Ni Houlihan for five years until I came across you.

* * * * *

Mr Belton: I can tell the Deputy the name of a man who last week bought two two-year-old cattle at £6 – £3 a head, a price that would be paid for them two years ago when they were dropped calves.
Mr Smith: They must have been smoking tobacco.

* * * * *

Mr O'Reilly: . . . If we only had sufficient power, there is not one in the House but would be the Cromwell – not one.

* * * * *

Mr Belton: . . . The minister had the audacity to get up and say that we would now have cheap food.
Mr O'Leary: And wide doors.

* * * * *

Mr McGilligan: . . . I have searched through Naas and I have not yet succeeded in getting an ordinary native sausage, let alone the delicatessen. Let me read what the Minister said about the factory on the occasion of its opening. It was described as 'the Viennese sausage factory'. There has always to be a touch of musical comedy associated with these new factories. . . .

* * * * *

4. Mid-Thirties

Mr O'Donovan: Is it not also a fact that (the man), who has got the appointment, has a charge pending against him for breaking windows in Glandore?
Mr Boland: I have no information on the matter.
Mr Dillon: All he knows is that he is a member of the Fianna Fáil Club!
Mr Boland: I beg to inform the Deputy that I have information that people on the other side are doing a lot of those things too – all over Cork.

*   *   *   *   *

Mr Fitzgerald: (The opposition) . . . reminded me of the Emperor of Abyssinia, who wanted to see a railway train, and who, when the train was drawn up before him at a certain place, looked at it and said: 'I thought it was bigger.'

*   *   *   *   *

Mr MacEntee: . . . I know that Deputy Dillon –
Mr Dillon: L'audace, toujours l'audace!
Mr MacEntee: – is already beginning to look a little like a splash headline in the *Independent*. . .
Mr Lemass: Those debts were not liquid – they froze.
Mr Belton: They froze afterwards. They are mummified since the Minister and his Government came in,
Mr S. Jordan: Wait for the thaw.
Mr Belton: Nothing will thaw them now, not even the sunny smile of the Minister. . .

*   *   *   *   *

Mr Lemass: There are four wireless stations in the country – Athlone, Dublin, Cork and Deputy Dillon. If Deputy Morrissey wants to be recognised as the fifth he will have to send in his application on the usual form.

*   *   *   *   *

Mr Norton: He has a scheme of his own – a new Italian scheme.

Mr Davin: Ice cream.

Mr Norton: If the ice were on the leader's head when he was making those statements there would be less nonsense in them.

* * * * *

Mr Mac Entee: Glamour is a word that has been used frequently in this debate. I think it used to be associated with the poets of the Celtic twilight. Now, we are having it associated with politicians of the Cumann na nGaedheal eclipse, the glamour of trade unionism. . .

* * * * *

Mr Dillon: . . . We must return again to the moderation and peace and conciliation of the Minister for Finance who, speaking at Navan, said:

> Knaves and traitors stand aside,
> Way for Ireland, Faugh a Ballagh.

Then we have the Minister for Finance at Mallow saying:

> Deputy MacDermot is one of the old Whig Castle Catholics with his puppy-dogs Belton, Cussen and O'Shaughnessy, arm in arm, breast high for England, every one of them trying to get into the good graces of England.

That is conciliation, peace and unity in politics.

Mr Lemass: I did not ask for any of these things. I ask only to turn from the sewage.

Mr Dillon: To turn off the sewage and to plunge into the Liffey at ebb tide. I think it is deplorable that we have to go through this ocean of slush which has poured down from Fianna Fáil platforms in the last two years. . .

* * * * *

Uniform (Restriction) Bill evoked this comment:

Mr Norton: . . . Deputy Fitzgerald proceeded to quote from a Papal Encyclical – not merely to quote from it but he proceeded to twist and pervert it. One would imagine from the quotation and from the meanings he purported to attach to them that a Papal Encyclical was written in order to justify the wearing of blue shirts. The whole purpose of his quotations was to show that many years ago His Holiness the Pope wrote a Papal

Encyclical justifying the wearing of blue shirts in the Saorstát in the year 1934. Is not that the most arrant nonsense that ever anybody tried to pass over on intelligent Deputies in this House? Not content with twisting and perverting the Encyclical, he went on to quote St Thomas Aquinas and one would imagine that St Thomas Aquinas was specially charged with the responsibility of justifying the wearing of blue shirts in the Irish Free State in 1934. . .

*   *   *   *   *

Mr Corry: . . . Deputy Byrne and some of them here think the whole of the Free State is in Dublin. It is not.
A Deputy: It is in Cork.

*   *   *   *   *

Mr Belton: . . . The producers of sheepskins are not in such circumstances that they can look forward to becoming millionaires either in this world or in the next. . .
Mr Belton: So you propose to buy the sheep without the skins?
Mr Lemass: A very large number of them. In fact, I think it is the regular practice in most civilised homes to eat the sheep without the skins.

*   *   *   *   *

Mr Belton: . . . The butcher will look for a licence, but the local Fianna Fáil Cumann will be acquainted and they will be asked what foot does the butcher dig with, and if he does not dig with the Fianna Fáil foot he will get no licence, any more than the feeders of fat cattle will get licences.
Mr T. Kelly: They might dig with the two feet.
Mr Belton: Ah, it will take you to do that, Tom.

*   *   *   *   *

Mr Lemass: For the information of the Deputy, sheepskins are not got from cattle.
Mr Dillon: When did the Minister learn that?
Mr Lemass: I mention it for the Deputy's information.
Mr Dillon: I thought that, perhaps, the Minister had been farming in his own constituency recently, cutting hay on the roofs of the houses and sowing wheat on Aran Quay.
Mr Belton: And the prairies of Cork Hill.
Mr Dillon: Yes, and the pastures of Patrick Street. . .

*   *   *   *   *

Dr Ryan: What I am trying to explain. . . is that we do not intend, and never hoped, to export every beast in the country in one fortnight.

Mr Keating: But what are we to do with the remaining 58 per cent of the cattle if the British will not have them?

Dr Ryan: We will eat them ourselves.

* * * * *

Mr Dillon: . . . If half the enthusiasm for proving that we are traitors and are playing England's game were put into the task of reviving the Irish language it would do. . . There are a lot of people romping around this country prepared to bawl 'Up, de Valera' and 'Up, the Republic,' but when you ask them are they prepared to do some really hard work they fade out of the picture; they wrap the green flag around them and vanish into the green wood.

Mr Smith: Kathleen Mavourneen.

Mr Dillon: That is what a lot of us are beginning to think, that the revival of Irish is a Kathleen Mavourneen revival – it may be for years and it may be for ever.

(Later)

Mr MacDermot: . . . I find that even in towns, on the occasion of political demonstrations, when the people are parading about the streets and want to sing something, they do not know any Gaelic melodies to sing. You hear them singing the 'Soldier's Song' without knowing the words, as a rule; and of course the 'Soldier's Song' has nothing Gaelic about it. Or you hear them even singing songs like 'Daisy Bell'. How that music-hall song of the nineties comes to be alive in Ireland I do not know. You hear them singing 'Daisy, Daisy, give me your answer do,' which has nothing to do with any political issue. . .

* * * * *

Mr Dillon: The Minister. . . has got Deputy Norton behind him, roaring like a lion ready for the fray. Let him take heart of courage.

Mr Boland: That is better then bellowing like an ass, is it not?

Mr Dillon: I described it politely; I do not necessarily say truthfully. . .

* * * * *

General Mulcahy: Will the Minister say if a man with seven years' service in the army, four years' service in the reserve – character 'Very Good' – and with four years' service in the reserve to go, has been discharged from the reserve and given no reason, good, bad or indifferent?

Mr Aiken: He was given a reason.

General Mulcahy: Was he given any other reason than that his services were no longer required by the Minister?

Mr Aiken: That, as I told the Deputy, is a very good reason. It was the reason for which the Deputy was kicked out of the Cabinet a few years ago.

*   *   *   *   *

Mr Corry: . . with regard to the last election, I did not need the help of the Knights of Columbanus.

Mr Anthony: On a point of order, Sir, what is the use of introducing Columbanus or anybody else?

An Leas-Cheann Comhairle: I do not understand the reference.

Mr Morrissey: Neither does the Deputy.

Mr Corry: Nor does St Anthony, I suppose.

*   *   *   *   *

Mr MacDermot: May I ask the Minister if he has given consideration to the amount of additional popularity acquired by Scottish Highland regiments in consequence of their kilts and whether there is any sound reason for denying to our Army that element of picturesqueness?

Mr Aiken: I think the Deputy will be in kilts then.

Mr Everett: What about the Blue Shirts wearing them?

*   *   *   *   *

Mr Corry: . . . I will admit that after the Intermediate examinations there came a change in our lives. Our parents decided that they would put us in different walks of life. Deputy Fitzgerald's parents, seeing what kind of a lackalally he was, thought that he could best earn his living by making daubs on paper. The only merit of his work, I think, was that you could not distinguish whether they were daubs of animals or of human beings. . .

*   *   *   *   *

Mr Belton: Name the countries in which conditions are worse then they are here.

Mr Lemass: The Isle of Man.

* * * * *

Mr Belton: Evidently my remarks are so soothing to some Deputies that they will slumber upon them, but there are other Deputies whom my remarks get on the raw, and who are not going to sleep upon them; and I shall continue for fear of their going to sleep. . .

* * * * *

Mr Davin: Is it in order for this big drummer to be passing remarks that are unparliamentary? . . .

Mr Anthony: We do not mind Deputy Davin, the flute player of the Fianna Fáil band here.

* * * * *

Mr Fitzgerald: . . I am quite certain that if Deputy Donnelly were putting forward a case for the canonisation of President de Valera, he would have, in President de Valera's speeches, ample evidence to justify that canonisation. I remember, some years ago, a man in the employ of the President brought out a book called *The One Hundred Best Sayings of President de Valera.* I, at the time, thought of bringing out *The One Hundred Second Best Sayings.*

* * * * *

Mr Donnelly: Will you give us the Irish of your own name?

Mr Belton: All I know about my name is that we did not come in the 'good ships gallantly from the sunny lands of Spain'. I do not care where the Beltons come from.

General Mulcahy: Matz, Lucks, Silverstein.

* * * * *

The President: . . . We all know the pulley and the bucket that is used for lifting up cement. I can imagine a few of those regular fellows there, having hoisted one of their companions a pretty good distance with the rope, sneering at him when he was at the top, saying: 'If you object to the position, why can you not loose yourself, by cutting the rope?'

* * * * *

Mr McMenamin: The Atlantic Ocean. . . Deputy Lynch, in his speech last night, mentioned certain proceedings of the Moville Board of Conservators and that while the meeting was going on. . . the *Muirchu* was at the south of the country while the board of Conservators were meeting at the north of the country. It reminded me of a *Life of Napoleon* that I once read, where it described the time when Napoleaon was in Egypt and the French fleet was destroyed. Napoleon had no way of getting home, and everybody thought that he was a prisoner and could not get back. Nelson was in the Mediterranean with the British fleet at the time. Napoleon succeeded in making his way home and afterwards there were cartoons in the comic papers of the time showing Nelson on the deck of a warship flirting with Lady Hamilton while Napoleon in a small boat was getting around the coast and home to France. I was reminded of that story when I heard the description of the depredations of the trawler around the coast up there while the *Muirchu* was in harbour. Probably the officers were flirting with the maidens of Killybegs.

*   *   *   *   *

Dr O'Higgins: . . . It was what I call a particularly slippy speech. We had that type of hair-splitting and phrase-splitting from beginning to end; we had the wriggle about Fianna Fáil promises –
Mr Briscoe: It was no wriggle.
Dr O'Higgins: And we had the challenge associated with the wriggle.
Mr Briscoe: The wriggle was over there.

*   *   *   *   *

Mrs Concannon: I did not intend to intervene in this debate, partly from a feeling of delicacy – my own interests being concerned – partly from the conviction that questions involving major issues of our Party's policy are best left to be defined and defended by our Front Bench. But when the Bill was in Committee, Deputy McGilligan gave me such a cordial invitation – which was repeated today by Deputy O'Sullivan – to take part in the discussion that I had not the heart to turn it down. It is true that the Deputy always likes to heighten the flavour of his cordials from the cayenne pepper castor, rather than with the other ingredients of the spice box. But, doubtless, that only makes them the more stimulating and piquant to the Northern palate. The Deputy and I, if not Arcadians both –

Arcades ambo – are the next best thing. We were both born in County Derry, and the pacifists, for that reason, nearly all belong to the company of which Deputy Dillon is a sworn brother:

We don't want to fight
But, by Jingo, if we do –

Deputy McGilligan has made a serious charge against me. He has accused me in the third person plural of having 'almost abolished myself by my performance in this House'. . .

*   *   *   *   *

Mr Corry: It is not the first time that that hound has hurled it across the house at me and it was hurled back in his teeth, the dying mongrel.

*   *   *   *   *

Mr Belton: . . . if the State comes to the rescue by inflating our barley price by five shillings a barrel. . . the taxpayer will have to provide that five shillings and of that five shillings the agricultural community will have to provide four.
Mr Davin: What about Guinness?
Mr Corry: There is no doubt, judging from Deputy Belton's speeches here, he is getting so bitter that he must be taking too much of his own rhubarb without sugar. . .
Mr Belton: The season is over now.
Mr Corry: You must be taking it out of season.

*   *   *   *   *

Mr Kelly: . . . If he had pronounced the word 'books' correctly I would have understood that he was referring to me. I thought the Deputy said second-hand boots.

*   *   *   *   *

Mr Belton: Nobody, neither the Minister nor anybody else, could buy me at any price. The Minister is here and he followed a Party that he knew were doing wrong and he followed them in the hope of getting office. The Minister is there –
Dr Ryan: And Deputy Belton is there where he is because we would not have him.
Mr Belton: I am here because I would not have you.
Mr Jordan: Are you all there?

Mr Belton: Sure, and well there.
Dr Ryan: It is well for us, anyway, that you are there.

* * * * *

Mr Curran: Nobody knows who these inspectors are or what their qualifications will be or anything else about them. Deputy Bennett says he hopes there will be men qualified to fill the position. I do not know.
Mr Corry: The inspector will not be like the tailor who came around to examine my bulls.

* * * * *

Dr Ryan: There was a practice some years ago in this country of giving a beggarman meal instead of money. Was the beggarman buying meal?
Mr Belton: The Minister is not thinking of the beggarman of Emyvale. He was begging for meal at Emyvale, and after a day there he got up on the hill outside and, looking down at Emyvale, said:

> Dear Emyvale, dear Emyvale,
> If you were as free from sin
> As you are from 'male,'
> You'd be happy Emyvale.

* * * * *

Mr Belton: The Minister understands the way that a butcher handles the products of a beast in order to get rid of them. Would he require to have a manufacturer's licence for that?
Dr Ryan: No.
Mr Belton: Is the Minister certain that a sausage would not be included? As well as meat you have other ingredients in it.
Mr Bennett: In Cork they are very fond of drisheen, which is made of blood.
Mr Belton: Would black pudding come under the section?
Dr Ryan: No, unless sold in a bottle.

5. Across the Floor

Irreverent snatches taken out of context in this section belie the enormous amount of constructive argument that took place in the second decade of Dáil Éireann.

*   *   *   *   *

Mr Lemass: Under the existing law there is no requirement that a person in charge of a boiler should have any particular competence for that class of work. . . .

*   *   *   *   *

When Mr Aiken, Minister for Defence stated that it was proposed to incorporate the O.T.C. in the Volunteer force he was challenged.
Mr Dockrell: When will the details of that be published?
Mr Aiken: Shortly, I hope.
Mr Dockrell: What does 'shortly' mean?
Deputies: Not long.

*   *   *   *   *

Mr Dillon: . . . I have heard, from any number of districts, that men have been told – not officially, but nevertheless, effectively – that if they join the local Fianna Fáil Cumann and pay their shilling, they will get work, and that if they do not join they will not get work.
Mr Flinn: A woman told me that a woman told her.

*   *   *   *   *

Mr Corry: . . . I know that in the town of Middleton, in the town of Cobh, and in the town of Youghal, the Labour Exchanges are manned by ex-members of the National Army –
Mr Jordan: Who are not members of Fianna Fáil, I presume.
Mr Corry: – who are very strong supporters of, and come out at every election to support, the other Party. I cannot imagine that those people are going to say:'He is a Fianna Fáil man and we will give him the job, and that another man is – I do not know what we can call him now – Blue Shirt, Black Shirt, or

Red, Black and Blue Shirt.
Mr Flinn: Call him a split pea.
Mr Corry: Or a split shirt. . . .

*   *   *   *   *

Mr Corry: . . . I have seen the girls who have been in that factory
for a year and a half and the lowest wages they are earning are
from 35/- to £2 16s 0d per week. These are not bad wages. It
reflects great credit on those who started the factory and started
it after being refused a Government loan.
Mr Dillon: What are they making?
Mr Corry: Come down and I will show you. I will show you a
lot of things you never saw before. I would nearly show you
Sing Sing if you came down.
Mr Dillon: What a fascinating creature!
Mr Corry: I am sure the Deputy would have to be very
fascinating before he would get out of it. . . .

*   *   *   *   *

Mr Flinn: The contribution from the local authority is always
considered the bull point in relation to applications for a grant.
Mr Belton: Well, we attempted it last year, and we did not score
any bull's eye.
Mr McGilligan: Bulls are cheaper this year.

*   *   *   *   *

Mr Lemass: The Deputy ought to be indignant. He is associated
with Deputy Dillon, but apparently he likes to lie in the same
sink with him. Deputy Dillon, no doubt, has dragged Deputy
Mulcahy down into it.
General Mulcahy: I am not the slightest bit indignant at the
stench.
Mr Lemass: If the Deputy cannot get the stench he is not very
sensitive.
Mr Dillon: You mean the stench of your red herrings?

*   *   *   *   *

Mr McGilligan: Unfortunately, your tongue slipped. . . .
Mr MacEntee: If my tongue slipped, my mind did not.
Mr McGilligan: We know you have a tongue, but as to the other —

*   *   *   *   *

Mr Dillon: . . . I think the Minister was on his feet four years ago and is on his head now. I can only hope that he will turn another somersault and land on his feet.

* * * * *

Mr Gilligan: . . . when is a blade a blank?
A Deputy: When it is a Deputy!
Mr McGilligan: Is it a fact that members of the Free State Army are shaving themselves with razors stamped 'Made in Britain', which are supposed to have been either manufactured or sharpened, or polished, or blunted, or something, here? Has the Minister ever heard any complaints with regard to that?
Mr Lemass: No.
Mr McGilligan: . . . The story I have heard is, that a certain firm did get into this particular production – whether sharpening or manufacturing I do not know – but they had a contract and managed to sell, at one-third over the contract price to the unfortunate soldiers of this country, razor blades supposed to be of Irish manufacture or finish, but all bearing the stamp of 'Made in Britain', and that stamp, despite other sharpenings or whatever it is that may have been put on, has not come off yet. The people concerned, the Minister told us, are a Belfast firm. I do not know who is registered in the companies office. I will see one of these days, but again I am told that the people who operate it are two, in the main. One is a gentleman who came to this country from Palestine *via* Great Britain and the other is a man who came from Belfast *via* Tanderagee – and they are a fairly good combination to manufacture Irish razor blades.
Mr Davin: Blunt ones!
Mr McGilligan: I do not notice the Army's appearance having deteriorated since these blades came in, but I know that their tempers are frayed.

* * * * *

Mr Flinn: . . . again the Deputy is walking hand-in-hand with me down this pleasant boreen.
Mr Curran: We have got to be great friends.

* * * * *

An Ceann Comhairle: The Deputy will repeat the words used.
Mr Corry: I said he was a 'sublimated idiot'.

An Ceann Comhairle: The Deputy must withdraw that remark.
Mr Corry: I will withdraw it. I will say he was talking blatherskite.

Mr Victory: On a point of order. What is the difference between that and the word 'amadaun' used by Deputy Dillon the other evening?
An Ceann Comhairle: That is not a point of order.
Mr Anthony: The only point is that 'amadaun' is Irish and you can say anything you like in Irish here because nobody else understands it.

*   *   *   *   *

Mr Ó Ceallaigh: We have no record of anybody dying of starvation during the period of office of this Government.

*   *   *   *   *

Mr Donnelly: We prefer human beings to bullocks. . . .

*   *   *   *   *

Mr Lemass: . . . we will want some place in which to keep wandering asses.
Mr Belton: We never had more jackasses or nanny goats in this country than now.
Mr Lemass: Jackasses are wandering about.
Mr Belton: There are a lot of them wandering about on the political platforms now throughout the country.
Mr Lemass: That is what we want the pounds for.

*   *   *   *   *

Mr Belton: . . . it will be news to Deputy Bennett to hear that we, in Dublin, must keep a wash basin, clean water, soap and a towel in the cowshed.
Mr Bennett: I do it myself.

*   *   *   *   *

Mr Cosgrave: If a Scotsman pays 520 guineas for a bull, it must be worth it. Would you not think so?
Dr Ryan: . . . the Scotsman knows more than we do about the thing.

*   *   *   *   *

Dr Ryan: The Deputy may try to run away from the chief argument which he used in his speech – farmyard manure.

* * * * *

Mr Dillon: I hope that the Minister will bear the graveyard in mind.

Mr Ó Ceallaigh: Unfortunately, I always do bear the graveyard in mind.

Mr Dillon: Does the Minister mean the graveyard of political reputations?

* * * * *

Mr Corry: . . . I am not going to mention Brian Boru except that I hope the Parliamentary Secretary will not do what was suggested and take him up in his aeroplane.

Mr Belton: Brian Boru was a good flier.

* * * * *

Mr Belton: What is a freshly-calved cow worth?

Dr Ryan: From £12 to £15.

Mr Belton: What is an old stripper worth?

* * * * *

Mr Dillon: What is going to become of the peat sacks?

Mr Lemass: They are still in use.

Mr Dillon: As bathing costumes in the bogs?

* * * * *

Mr Dillon: Bonhams. You would not call them 'bawneens' unless you put them on.

Mr Keogh: We call them bonneens. I am not a purist.

* * * * *

Mr Belton: I do not bet. I never put a bob on a horse in my life. But if you know exactly where you are going it takes the whole spice out of life. . . There is nothing like an element of risk. That is the only thing worth having in this life.

Mr McGilligan: That is a bad phrase for a politician – getting tired of running in a straight line.

Mr Belton: There are not many straight political lines in this country. I do not think Euclid was a politician.

Mr McGilligan: We have a mathematical President at the moment.

Mr Belton: Euclid was not a politician because if he were he would never define what a straight line was.

* * * * *

During the taking of a Resolution, threads and yarns were being discussed.

Mr Belton: You did not start spinning the yarns yet, but there is a 40 per cent duty on them.

Mr Lemass: I should like to put a very heavy duty on some of the jokes we hear in this House, jokes which are by no means original.

* * * * *

Mr MacDermot: . . . The United Party is a new Party. It contains elements that were never in the Cumann na nGaedheal Party.

Mr Donnelly: What is the title of it. United Ireland?

Mr MacDermot: Yes.

Mr Donnelly: That is why there are so many splits.

Mr Norton: Chips.

* * * * *

Mr J. M. Burke: . . . I forgive the President many things, but I find it very hard to discover any excuse for his having sanctioned. . . the use of that mongrel word 'Seanascal' as the title of the so-called Governor-General, who, by the way, is wrapped in the cloak of darkness. I object to the word on various grounds. In the first place it is suspiciously suggestive of 'Seanasal'. In the second place it is a mere Gaelic adaptation of an English word 'Seneschal', which in turn is derived from two German words which mean 'an old servant', . . . it is very hard precisely to understand what it does signify.

An Ceann Comhairle: I should like to draw the Deputy's attention to the fact that the Governor-General is not 'the so-called Governor-General'. Secondly, the name 'Seanascal' has been there for years and the President is not responsible for the title.

* * * * *

Mr Kelly: . . . The President is black as black could be. He is ebon black, a white spot cannot get through. His Ministers are all black. I do not know what the back benchers are as black as. . . .

* * * * *

Mr Kelly:. . . . A Deputy opposite, speaking here the other night, said that somebody told him that the Fianna Fáil back benchers were all living tombstones. When I heard him say that I stretched myself to see if I were flattened out. I have not much room to stretch here, but I felt the tombstone all over me. . . I do not think that we are the type of jockeys that the Aga Khan would employ to ride his winners. We would be too heavily weighted with precipices round our necks and tombstones hanging out of our eyebrows. The country is ruined. . . wirrastrue.

* * * * *

Mr Belton: . . . If this debate is going to develop into one on general agricultural policy, I will have to ask permission to be allowed to speak again in order to cover a wider field.

* * * * *

Mr Hogan: . . . For some years past the Abbey Theatre has been endeavouring to make the Irish peasant stand on his head. We are granting £1,000 to a theatre which has very limited appeal.

* * * * *

Mr O'Leary: I will never leave Cork until the last day. I love the county. They are very sane people down there.
Mr Corry: I wish you had stopped with them a little longer. . . .

* * * * *

Mr Lemass: I read in the papers last week that the American boxer who entered the ring with Jack Doyle was only 17 years of age, and people of that kind must be considered as well as the tender, delicate people about whom Deputy Norton is concerned.
Mr Norton: This Bill does not concern boxers.
Mr Lemass: I think I would prefer to do any sort of hard work than enter the ring against a boxer like Jack Doyle. . . .

* * * * *

Mr McGilligan: . . . I thought Deputy Smith was going to break silence again. I am sure he has heard of the heroic type of sentimental novel where the hero and the heroine get lost in the great wide spaces. Nearly all around is silence, and after a bit they think they alone are alive in a world that is otherwise dead.

Mr MacEntee: And there is one man on the ice floe.

*   *   *   *   *

Minister for Industry and Commerce (Mr Lemass): There is no tax on footballs: only on football covers. The wind is still free of duty.

Mr Fitzgerald-Kenney: I would like to see a football without a cover.

Mr Bennett: I do not know what made the Minister for Finance pick on footballs for this tax. There was a time, perhaps, when some Fianna Fáil Deputies played football with part of the intestines of a pig. Perhaps the Minister intends to drive people back to that crude method of enjoyment, by taxing leather covers.

*   *   *   *   *

Mr Bennett: What I am surprised at is that the Irish air is not being taxed. . . I suggest that one way of improving this industry here would be to buy a few footballs and to get some of the Deputies on the back benches opposite to take part in a match. . . They might be profitably engaged in playing football on the lawn when they are not taking part in the debates. At an rate, it would be physical exercise for them.

A Deputy: Will you select a team to meet us?

Mr Bennett: A team can be selected from amongst the Deputies opposite. I daresay some of them have played the game. . . .

*   *   *   *   *

Mr Lemass: There is no tax on bladders.

Mr Bennett: I refrained from using that word in the House. I did not think we should name such intestines.

Mr Belton: We have 'blathers' for export.

*   *   *   *   *

Mr McGilligan: . . . on the back of the Pigs Bill ride the tyres and the ink.

A Deputy: And the cutlery.

Mr McGilligan: – and the cutlery on their passage, as far as this House is concerned, to the Statute Book tonight.

* * * * *

Mr Kelly: You are full of brass. . . .

Mr Belton: I would smother my face if it were half as brassy as yours.

Mr Corry: Keep it for the next election.

Mr MacEntee: He will have a little Fine Gael polish on it by then.

* * * * *

Mr Kelly: . . . I do not eat beef because I was told it was bad for the complexion. I was told that when I would become an old man I would be a very ugly man if I continued to eat beef, so I turned to mutton. . . it is possible that some day people may be able to do without food at all.

A Deputy: They will be able to live on air.

Mr Kelly: Exactly. We are told that the electrons in the air contain life-sustaining substances, and that all you need to do in future when you are hungry is to open your mouth –

A Deputy: And see what God will send you.

Mr Kelly: By simply opening your mouth, you will swallow some substance that will sustain life. . . .

* * * * *

Mr Belton: The bankrupt bullock will have to carry the whole lot.

* * * * *

Mr Cosgrave: . . . So far as my investigations go, the only person who can partially escape is a pilgrim in Lough Derg, because there is not yet a tax on salt, pepper or water. . . .

* * * * *

Mr Norton: . . . If any ill-digested phrase could be imagined. . . surely this is a classic example.

Mr Lemass: What is the Deputy's objection to it?

Mr Norton: A natural aversion to a foolish phrase.

Mr Lemass: He must have developed that during the Recess.

* * * * *

Mr Keyes: . . . If a man of the type I am referring to is to get his 15 minutes' rest, is it intended that he must sit down under the eye of his employer or foreman? What would be meant by 'the premises' in a case of that kind? . . . take the case of a railway company which wants to build a bridge. . . presumably, on a railway bridge the premises would be the bridge?

*   *   *   *   *

Mr J. M. Burke: . . . Dr Webb was a County Court Judge. He was a very distinguished graduate of Trinity College, and figured very prominently in the old Phoenix Park murder trials. Before his County Court some barrister quoted a case which had been decided on circuit by a very distinguished Judge. . . Dr Webb pulled his wig aside, and gave him a withering look. 'My dear young man,' he said, 'do not give me a Circuit Court decision, I have no doubt it was decided by a Judge who was rushing to catch the 3 o'clock train to go back to Dublin, and argued by two barristers who were drunk the night before, instructed by two solicitors who were always drunk.'

*   *   *   *   *

Mr Corry: You are a city representative.
Mr Belton: I farmed more land in ten years than you would farm in ten lifetimes.
Mr Corry: I am elected by farmers; you are not.
Mr Belton: Then I must apologise for the low intelligence of farmers, and I think I am wasting any intelligence I have in speaking on their behalf here if that is all they can elect.
Mr Corry: They were intelligent enough to kick you out anyway.

*   *   *   *   *

Speaking about Deputy Morrissey;
Mr Ó Ceallaigh: . . . It is a good job to hear his voice, even though we do hear the crocodile tears too.
Mr MacDermott: How does the Minister manage to 'hear' a tear?
Mr Ó Ceallaigh: I heard his voice.
Mr MacDermott: The Minister said he heard his tears.
Mr Ó Ceallaigh: . . . one could hear them falling and hopping off the benches. . . .

*   *   *   *   *

Mr Corry: . . . Deputies should be apprenticed out to good farmers like me who would teach them how to work and how to farm. I can assure them that after a period they will work all right.

Mr Finlay: I hope you will not put them into dairy farming. I would not like to see young fellows brought up dishonestly.

Mr Corry: I realise that you can get nothing from a pig but a grunt.

*　*　*　*　*

Mr Corry: . . . We appreciate ignorance when we see it. . . We hear Deputy Dillon, with all his sanctimonious expression of beautiful adjectives. . . talking about. . . the miserable Minister of Agriculture. . . so far as I can gather, the Deputy does all his farming in a flower box in a certain window in the city. He regards himself as an authority on farming as on everything under the sun. He is an authority on maize meal, on corrugated iron and corrugated buckets. . . .

*　*　*　*　*

Mr MacDermott: . . . Deputy Hogan (is) a speaker so delightful that, if it were in order, I should feel inclined to propose that a certain mat with 'Welcome' inscribed on it should be laid down every time he does us the favour of coming to the House. . . .

*　*　*　*　*

During the Motion to Elect Deputies to a Committee of Privilege, Mr Dillon delivered an oration and then left the chamber. He prompted a pair of analogies from an opponent:

Mr Flinn: . . . he. . . reminds me of a churchwarden in the divorce court, or the devil quoting Scripture.

*　*　*　*　*

Mr J. M. Burke: . . . no one would put Thersites or Cleon on the same pedestal with the President. . . No one would think of comparing Annanias with our respected Vice-President and surely no one would dream of comparing Cacus, the cattle stealer, with the Minister for Agriculture. . . no one would back Tom Thumb against Eugene Sandow and no one would pit the Hunchback of Notre Dame against Dan O'Mahoney. . . .

*　*　*　*　*

A report in the *Herald Examiner* was read in the chamber.

Mr T. Kelly: 'Boob-Boopa-Doop girl on way to Reno. Miss Helen Dane', the film actress, who became known as the "Boopa-Doop Girl" because of a phrase she coined, is on her way to Reno to start divorce proceedings... She is quoted as saying that she has no special complaint, but that she and her husband, Mr Max Hoffman, junior, are "incompatible". They were married in February the 1st, 1933.'

You will notice that the paper says 'in' instead of 'on'. That indicates that the writer has got a university education. . . . -

*   *   *   *   *

Mr Corry: The Dublin Corporation was so corrupt they had to get a City Manager to manage their affairs.

Mr Norton: Is it in order to say that the Dublin Corporation is the most corrupt body in the Free State?

An Leas-Cheann Comhairle: A corporate body cannot be said to have a reputation.

*   *   *   *   *

Mr Brennan: . . . This Estimate really shows us the type of wibbly-wobbly, forlorn agricultural policy which the Government have. In the main Estimate last year we had an increase in salaries and wages of £23,081. In this Estimate we have a further increase in salaries and wages. What have we got for that increase?

Mr Belton: The warble fly.

*   *   *   *   *

Mr Belton: . . . A Deputy behind me says the farmers are burst. If they are, they have only to thank themselves because 50 per cent. of them put the Government in here on the promise that they would settle the economic war. . . after I have finished here I have to interview a man in whose house the sheriff is at the moment –

Mr Kennedy: Better hurry up; he will not wait for you.

Mr Belton: That is a matter for laughter here. . . They are on the way to a man who was on the Minister's platform in the last election but he will never be such a fool as to be there again. . . Perhaps it is a godsend, a blessing in disguise, that the accumulated stupidity of the Ministry produced this abortion, the coal-cattle pact, and that it will provide the epitaph which,

on some glorious day, we shall write on the tomb over the Fianna
Fáil Government – 'R.I.P. Killed by the second dose of the coal-
cattle pact. . .'

*　*　*　*　*

Dr Ryan: . . . Deputy Cosgrave. . . went to talk of his two
favourite subjects, finance and horse-breeding. He gave us a
lecture about sterling blocks and non-sterling blocks, about
dollar blocks and gold blocks and so on.
Mr Donnelly: And blockheads.
Mr Brennan: No, he left that out.
Mr Dillon: Yes, he left it out. He did not notice the Minister on
the Front Bench.

*　*　*　*　*

Mr Dillon: Deputy O'Reilly was put up as a stalking horse. He
was given the dirty job to do. And he came in here and made
a complete ass of himself.

*　*　*　*　*

Mr Anthony: . . . this is the kind of thing one hears at the cross-
roads – the eyes of the earth are on Ballymacscattery today.
There was once a little paper published in West Cork –
A Deputy: The *Skibbereen Eagle*.
Mr Anthony: And this little paper said, 'The eyes of the Eagle
are on the Czar of Russia.'

(To the present day there is controversy about that alleged
excerpt from the *Cork County Eagle and Munster Advertiser*,
to give the publication its correct title. The actual piece has never
been produced although later references to its use are available.)

*　*　*　*　*

Mr Aiken: . . . I have no control over Deputy McGilligan's
nostrils. To the badger the sweetest smelling rose in the world
just smells badger. To a pig that has been wallowing in his own
dirt the sweetest smelling rose in the world just smells pig
manure. And to Deputy McGilligan the most open, honourable
transaction in the world just has the stench of the excretion of
his own foul mind. . . one way that was common a few hundred
years ago of dealing with persons like Deputy McGilligan has

gone out of fashion, and all we can do is rely on the electors to use Keating's Powder. . . .

* * * * *

Mr MacDermot: Can the Deputy define jazz?
Mr Keogh: It seems to me to be a cross between a waltz and all-in wrestling. . .

* * * * *

Mr Boland: In dealing with Deputy McGilligan I must try to be charitable because I do not think he can help himself. . . Some people have remarked that they thought he was born that way but I think that would be in the nature of blasphemy. I think that the nurse put some vinegar in his milk when he was a baby and that he has been generating venom ever since. If he did not emit some of it now and again, he would collapse completely. I hope some of these explosions will do him good physically. . . .

* * * * *

Mr Finlay: . . . Let no one think that artificial manure is going to keep the heart in any land. It is like a person taking a half of whiskey or a half of rum. It may elevate him for the time being, but the effect is not lasting. . . .

* * * * *

Mr T. Kelly was told by a member of the Seanad that they were 'dying like gentlemen'.
Mr Kelly: He proved that by saying that they were going to die like the old French aristocrats who, when ascending the steps of the guillotine took off their hats and saluted that particular instrument. That member made a courtly bow, took off his hat to show how he would do it. I would have returned the bow myself only that I am a bit stiff in the back. . . .

* * * * *

General Mulcahy: . . . We had advertisements reminding the people that countless suns had crossed the sky since the elk roamed Ireland –
Mr Lemass: There are a few elks knocking around yet.
General Mulcahy: There are, and they are treading on people's toes just as the elks long ago, according to the Government propaganda. . . , trod the earth of Ireland into the sweetest-

smelling, the most useful and the loveliest fuel that was ever made. . . we were told how turf was formed through the countless ages by the tramp of Finn MacCool and his countless legions, by gallant Red Hugh and his legions. In fact the people were encouraged to buy turf even for literary purposes. . .

* * * * *

Mr Belton: A bad workman always blames his tools.
Mr Lemass: I am not quarrelling with the party opposite.

* * * * *

Mr MacEntee: . . . Let us hear no more from Deputy McGilligan about bribery and corruption, because when the Deputy opens his mind on that subject in this House, it is like removing the lid from a long-buried coffin.

* * * * *

General Mulcahy: . . . I oppose the putting on of an additional tax. . . on pepper. . . cloves, cinnamon, nutmeg, etc.
Mr Anthony: What about the ginger of the Labour Party.

* * * * *

Mr Dillon: . . . I wonder how many flannelette-lined boots are sold in this country.
Mr Lemass: How many flannelette-soled boots?
Mr Dillon: I have yet to hear that the manufacturers who are enjoying the Minister's protection can sole their boots with flannelette. We may hope to reach that stage yet, but I believe, however, that a scandal of that kind would stir up the country as to the value the Irish people are getting in this matter of flannelette-soled boots.
Mr Lemass: Paper soles.
Mr Dillon: There is no law against the making of paper-soled boots. That is a wider story. . . .

* * * * *

Mr McGilligan: If you kick the feet from under an infant you may put it on a sound basis. . . .

6. War on the Horizon

Mr J. M. Burke appealed to song writers to support Amendment
No. 20 to the 1936 Finance Bill. Then he quoted:

> It is little for glory I care;
> Ambition is only a fable.
> I'd as soon be meself as Lord May'r
> While there are lashings of stout on the table.

> Irish stout I have no doubt
> In either wood or bottle,
> And well brewed ale will never fail
> To cool a thirsty throttle.

The Deputy also gave a short version of the history of brewing
in Ireland, finishing with 'In ancient Ireland only peers were
brewers and, in modern Ireland, only brewers are peers.'

* * * * *

Mr Lemass: The Deputy has a habit of shutting his mouth after
he has put his foot in it.

* * * * *

A mixture of pepper and ginger on stout, was, according to one
Deputy, very popular in cold weather.
Mr J. N. Burke: . . . It is known in my part of the country as a
'shake of the lad'. For the future I am afraid the 'shake of the
lad' will become a thing of the past. . . .

* * * * *

There was disagreement about soldiers carrying out work
normally done by civilians at Custume Barracks, Athlone. The
Parliamentary Secretary to the Minister for Defence, Mr
Traynor, said it was an essential part of the training of military
units and received a retort.
Mr Davin: Is steam-rolling part of the ordinary training of
soldiers?

* * * * *

Mr Aiken: . . . If Deputy Fitzgerald-Kenney invited Deputy Dillon into his house and gave him a bed for the night, we do not want Deputy Dillon to claim the right to remain there and to take the bed away with him when going. . . .

* * * * *

Mr Fitzgerald-Kenney: That is an argument on the grounds of symmetry. . .On the same principle on which the Minister is going, if you have a bed that is too big you can stretch the gentlemen out so that he will be long enough to fit in the bed, or you can cut his legs off so that he will be short enough if the bed is a short one. . . .

* * * * *

Mr Derrig: . . . stunt flying and flying at low altitudes are forbidden. . . .
Mr Dillon: You must fly at a low altitude if you are going to land.

* * * * *

Mr Cosgrave: I want(ed) to know if the Minister claims to be in the state of grace since he took over office?
Mr Ó Ceallaigh: No, unfortunately; I wish I could say that. I am nearly always in the state of disgrace. . . .

* * * * *

Bacon was the subject for discussion when this question was asked:
Mr Keogh: Would you rather have them buying the 'lad'?
Mr Daly: I do not know what the Deputy means.
Mr Keogh: . . . In the previous régime, the labourers and farmers bought what was popularly known as the 'lad' – which is the pseudonym for American bacon – because they said it greased the cabbage.

* * * * *

Mr Dillon: . . . blood cannot be got from a turnip, water from a stone, or a quart out of a pint pot.
Mr Davin: What about a mug?

* * * * *

Mr Dillon: . . . if you are going to employ 100 people for the manufacture of toe-puffs and stiffeners, that is the eighth wonder of the world.

* * * * *

Mr Flinn: . . . We have just heard the expression 'sewer rat'. I challenge the suggestion that has been made that I started it.
Mr Norton: It is hardly fair to the rat.

* * * * *

Mr Lavery: . . . The President has said that the use of the words 'organ' or 'constitutional organ' is a more appropriate way of describing the King.

* * * * *

The Attorney General: . . . Deputy Costello at one time put forward the suggestion that the legislation. . . was going to create half a king.
Mr Costello: Half a Crown was the phrase.

* * * * *

Mr Dillon: . . . The supervision of whale fishing is a very expensive business. It means you have to put an inspector on every whaler. . . .
Mr MacDermot: Could not the warble fly inspectors be used for this purpose?

* * * * *

The erection of a new waiting room at Leinster House was being discussed when Mr Corry asked:
Mr Corry: I should like to know when you are going to remove the scarecrow in front of the entrance to Leinster House?
   (The allusion was to the statue of Queen Victoria, erected in 1908. It was removed eventually in 1948.)

* * * * *

Mr Keogh: . . . The houses that are proposed to be built on this site would stand on the grounds on which the Battle of Vinegar Hill was fought, a place of great repute in Irish history. Houses built there would have an historic interest. From the point of sanitary possibilities, the site is unique. It is high and dry. . . .

* * * * *

Dr Ryan defended the Government's record in taking taxes off essential foods.

Mr O'Leary: Have you taken anything off saucepans?

Dr Ryan: A saucepan is not an essential food.

* * * * *

Mr Finlay: . . . I do not want any assistance from Deputy Jordan.

Mr Jordan: You will not get it.

Mr Finlay: I do not require it.

Mr Jordan: You may find yourself on the rocks.

Mr Finlay: I am not on the rocks. I have a sounder keel than you can put up.

* * * * *

Mr Vincent Rice: What about (the Governor General's) pension? . . .

Mr McGilligan: There is nothing in that about his pension.

Mr Corry: Ah, no, there is not, nor about the £750 piano the Deputy's Government gave the last joker.

* * * * *

The President: . . . I have often been asking myself why it is that some people have been spreading the idea that I was somehow or other opposed to or have reactionary views about women. I have not, as far as I know, and I challenge anybody to show it, in public or private.

* * * * *

Mr MacDermot: . . . It seems to me to be mere make-believe to try to incorporate a word like 'Taoiseach' in the English Language.

* * * * *

Mr McGilligan: Of the three points in the amendment, sex is covered, religion lies over to a later clause, and class cannot be defined.

The President: That is the trouble with class.

* * * * *

Mr Corry: Apparently some of the heads over there are so thick that it requires a mallet to drive any facts into them.

Mr Brodrick: Give us something new.

* * * * *

Mr Lemass: . . . Apparently, when compiling the cost-of-living index, it is only streaky bacon they take into account.

*   *   *   *   *

Mr Dillon: . . . Now we know where we are.
Mr Flinn: Since when?

*   *   *   *   *

Mr Dillon: How can the natural resources of this country be compared with Sweden's timber. . . There are lunatic asylums in Sweden just as in Dublin.
Mr Briscoe: There are no Dillons over there.

*   *   *   *   *

Mr Lemass: In this Bill a wife is a relative.
Mr Fitzgerald-Kenney: I do not think that that is at all clear.

*   *   *   *   *

The Committee Stage of the Presidential Seal Bill drew fire.
Mr O'Neill: Will the Minister say if the design will be open to competition among artists?
The President: I think that will not be necessary as we will be able to have most of the old design.
Mr Dillon: A change without a difference.
The President: No. We will keep the design, but the essential part will be changed.
Mr Norton: What will it be like?
Mr MacEntee: Would the Deputy like to substitute a loud speaker for the harp?
 Resolution agreed to.

*   *   *   *   *

Mr Norton: . . . the outstanding defect so far as cottages in the County Kildare are concerned is in the chimneys. . . Wherever the smoke goes in labourers' cottages in other counties, the fact remains that in Kildare the smoke will go anywhere but up the chimney. . . .

*   *   *   *   *

Mr Benson: . . . It seems to me that nothing in the Bill would prevent me from driving my car to the North Wall, if I was going across to England, and having the car refused shipment on the grounds that it was scrap iron. As there is no definition, some people might refer to it as 'scrap iron' while others might refer to it as 'a family heirloom'.

* * * * *

When the definition of a shop came up for discussion, Mr T. Kelly wondered what was the position about tinkers who sold horses:
Mr Dillon: I have yet to meet a shop which caters for horses. . . .

* * * * *

An Gúm's function of publishing works of literature in the Irish language was to be extended to cover music. The Minister for Education explained:
Mr Derrig: . . . the intention is to publish arrangements or settings of original Irish airs as far as possible. I dare say that if a new composer sails into our ken, who is capable of doing for native Irish music what has been done in other countries by composers of the present day or the Russian composers of some time back, it would be a question whether such a composer would be passed as being really true to the Irish genius or whether he had forsaken the native music for modern modes. . . .
Mr Dillon: An Gúm passing judgement on Sibelius!

* * * * *

Mr O'Neill: A refreshment house is a hotel, according to the definition, but a hotel is not a refreshment house.
Mr Fitzgerald-Kenney: Some refreshment houses are hotels, but all refreshment houses are not hotels.
Mr O'Neill: The word 'hotel' does not include a refreshment house, but a refreshment house includes a hotel.

* * * * *

Mr McMenamin: . . . you see a little boy or girl of 11, 12, 13 or 14 years of age carrying a bag of books about three times the size of the dispatch bag that a university professor would carry.
Mr Davin: We presume that the professor would not have to carry a bag; he would carry it all in his head.
Mr McMenamin: . . . I am speaking of the average child, and, after all, we must deal with the average person in this House. How is the average child to get any real grasp –
Mr Corish: Of the bag?

* * * * *

The International Convention for the Regulation of Whaling was signed in Geneva in 1931. The Minister for Agriculture referred to it in March 1938.

Mr Norton: What is the effect of it on the whales?

Dr Ryan: It is to preserve the whales.

Mr P. Hogan: And it took you seven years to do that.

Dr Ryan: It is a big subject.

* * * * *

Mr Ó Ceallaigh: . . . He has. . . never been able to get the smoke to go up the £3,500 chimney. . . He paid £3,500 for that house.

Mr McMenamin: Not for the chimney?

Mr Ó Ceallaigh: A chimney is an essential part of a house.

Mr O'Neill: He will have to cease supporting the Government.

* * * * *

Mr Dillon: . . . The Prime Minister is reported as saying: 'You and I are one, but I am the one'. This comes from an old story about a blushing bride. According to the story, the bridegroom remarked to the bride: 'You and I are one,' and the blushing bride replied: 'But I am the one.' I am quite prepared to welcome the Prime Minister's conversation but proposals of marriage are as yet a little embarrassing.

Mr Corish: No confetti now.

* * * * *

Mr McMenamin: Is a dog an agricultural product?

Dr Ryan: Oh, yes, certainly a dog is.

* * * * *

Mr Dillon: What is the meaning of taking the duty off rose bushes in reference No. 7 and putting it on again in reference No. 9 of Schedule 3?

Dr Ryan: That refers to rose stocks. They are different from rose bushes. Rose stocks are what the bushes are grafted on.

Mr Dillon: If I buy a rose bush from Samuel McGready of Portadown, is there a 2d. duty on it now?

Dr Ryan: 3d. That would be a rose bush.

Mr Dillon: Are you not taking the duty off rose bushes?

Dr Ryan: No. We are reducing it from 6d. to 3d.

Mr Dillon: You are taking the duty off rose stocks altogether?

Dr Ryan: Yes, if they are of United Kingdom origin.

Mr Moore: 'A rose by any other name. . .'

* * * * *

Mr Hogan: . . . because of some trade unionists who swallow slogans at election times and may one day realise that a dictator has got into the saddle and trade unionism has got to take its place behind him.

Mr Linehan: In the saddle also?

Mr Hogan: Not in the sadddle, but in the procession.

Mr Flinn: The metaphor is nearly as confused as the horse.

Mr Hogan: My metaphors are understandable. My figures of speech are few, and, if I were to create a figure of speech to describe the Parliamentary Secretary, it would not be at all mixed. . .

* * * * *

Mr Dillon: . . . Art silk is coming into this country from Japan at 4d. a yard, 6d. in check, 4d. in plain colours. In the country little girls, and big girls, buy it for dance frocks and for Sunday frocks.

Mr Heron: And little girls make it in Japan.

* * * * *

Mr Davin: . . . Deputy Corry does not do much damage to the road from Cork to Dublin. I believe he travels mostly by rail.

Mr Corry: I try to keep you going.

Mr Davin: Keep me on the rails anyway.

Mr McGowan: It is a pity there is a railway from Cork to Dublin.

* * * * *

The following remarks were made during a discussion on the economic war:

Mr Gorey: The farmers have stood up to the fight, but the Minister was not in the trenches; he was never asked to go into the trenches. The position is that he flung one regiment into the trenches and left them there all the time.

Mr Mac Entee: Was the Deputy in the trenches?

Mr Gorey: Yes, all the time.

Mr Mac Entee: Well, then, he will appreciate the words of the old song, 'Johnny, I hardly knew you.'

Mr Keating: Johnny, you hardly know yourself.

* * * * *

Mr Dockrell: Some months ago I bought an Irish spade and used it for the purpose for which it was designed. It was not long before I noticed the laminations in the spake (undoubtedly a. misprint) parting company and presently a bit came off. A little bit later on the handle broke. I brought the handle with me. Here is the handle (produced).

Mr Victory: A very dangerous weapon.

The discussion continued with remarks such as 'The Deputy wants to shovel them out of existence' and 'I do not want them to dig themselves in. . .' It ended with the following:

Mr Tubridy: You want to go four spades on a two spade hand.

Mr Dockrell: I think I have the ace of spades.

*   *   *   *   *

Mr Aiken: . . . In accordance with ordinary international custom and Army regulations, when I invited certain British officers to dinner in Cork, to return some of the courtesy which they had shown our people when they were engaged in negotiations as to the handing over of the ports, I proposed the health of the head of their State, and, in return, their senior officer proposed the health of the head of our State. That is all that happened.

Mr McMenamin: The King's health.

Mr Aiken: I proposed it in Irish first and then in English.

Capt.Giles: And the King got sick in the meantime.

Mr Gorey: It turned his stomach.

Mr Aiken: I am quite prepared to drink his health every time he hands over a lump of territory, and if he hands over the Six Counties, I will drink his health six times. . .

*   *   *   *   *

Mr Dillon: . . . a country woman's idea of washing an egg usually is to get water at a temperature which will melt the dirt, but unfortunately (this) will also boil the egg. . . , it is not easy to recognise a washed egg unless you candle it. You cannot candle every egg on the side of the road.

*   *   *   *   *

Dr Ryan: . . . I do not want to compete against Deputy Belton in religious doctrine, but I heard him talking about the Reds eating our bulls in Barcelona.

Mr Belton: That is a bull they will never eat.

*   *   *   *   *

As war clouds began to gather over Europe, concern for safety was growing.

Captain Giles: . . . We have heard a great deal about saving the people of Dublin from air raids. What are you saving in Dublin? A whole horde of wealthy men who have come from all parts of the world to enjoy what should be for the use and support of the Irish people themselves. . . We are asked to put up shelters for these men when we should be asked to build shelters for our own cattle which will help to bring prosperity to our country and to our own people.

Mr Belton: Hitler.

Captain Giles: I wish we had a Hitler for the defence of Ireland. . .

* * * * *

Mr Corry: . . . Everything that this Government has done must be wrong in Deputy Brasier's eyes. He views everything through red, white and blue glasses. . . .

* * * * *

The Minister for Posts and Telegraphs (Mr Traynor) was accused.

Mr Dillon: . . . His outlook and mind, as well as the outlook and mind of most of his colleagues, are circumscribed by the North Circular Road. Dublin is his end-all and be-all. So long as everything is rosy in the garden, so far, let us say, as Lucan, everything is all right.

* * * * *

Mr Morrissey described export bounties as feeding people with 'a bit of their own tail' and received the response:

Mr Ryan: Does the Deputy think that the Government could have paid these bounties by any other method than by feeding them with a bit of their own tail?

Mr Mac Entee: It is better than stuffing them with Fine Gael yarns.

* * * * *

During a discussion on The Offences Against the State Bill, 1939, the Lord Mayor of Cork was taken to task for expressing pride in the 'law-abiding citizens of his native city'. The admonishment continued:

Mr T. Kelly: . . . I wonder did he ever hear of a writer named Max O'Rell? Max O'Rell was a Frenchman who wrote travel books and he visited Ireland, and he visited Cork. (There) he got on an outside car and drove around the heights of Cork and the jarvey said to him, pointing away in the distance: 'Do you see that city' or 'that town'. 'Yes,' said Max O'Rell. Then the jarvey said to him: 'There are ten thousand men in that town ready to die for Ireland.' And Max O'Rell said: 'Why do they not do it?' The jarvey answered: 'The police would not let them.'
Mr Everett: Where are these Cork men now?
Mr T. Kelly: I expect they are law-abiding still. . .

*   *   *   *   *

Loans for farmers led to slaughtering of calves which Mr Belton felt would have been worth £10,000,000 if they had been held on to.
Mr Mac Entee: They would have been beef steaks before this.
Mr Belton: The Minister has secured his beef steak and his pension.
An Ceann Comhairle: If the Deputy desires to intervene, he will have an opportunity of doing so in an orderly manner.
Mr Moore: That is the last thing the Deputy wishes – to interfere in an orderly manner. He always rather enjoys trying to interfere with others. . . .

*   *   *   *   *

The Vote for the Office of the Minister for Education brought criticism about the 'little dog kennels of schools' that children had to attend.
Mr Dillon: . . . In or about 1835, you would have found in the back blocks or backwoods of North America the kind of national schools we have in this country, but there they have removed all these things to the museums now, and people can go and look at their models, with suitable backgrounds of attacking Indians painted on them, and so on, and of Buffalo Bills coming to protect them from attack. . . .

*   *   *   *   *

According to Mr Gorey, Mr Aiken's Volunteers would not fight. This almost led to a scrap on the floor.
Mr Aiken: The Deputy is an old man and I shall not –
Mr Gorey: You will get better fighters amongst the old men than

amongst the young men.

Mr Aiken: A lot of them will run after hares and do a bit of poaching but they will not do much more.

Mr Gorey: They ran after you.

Dr O'Higgins: Ran like hares.

* * * * *

Mr P. J. Fogarty claimed that children repeated their nursery rhymes in Irish even in North County Dublin, giving as examples 'Eeny, meeny, miny, mo' and 'Hi-diddle-diddle'.

Mr D. Morrissey: What is the Gaelic for 'Hi-diddle-diddle'?

Captain Giles: That is a 'bookie' term.

Mr Fogarty: And there might have been many a good horse of that name. There is a horse of the name of Blueshirt, too. . . .

Mr Morrissey: What are the odds?

Mr Fogarty: A tip for him came in a bottle down in Stradbally. . . .

* * * * *

Mr Moore: . . . The rubber boot is more than a boot – it is an ankle cover as well.

Mr Dillon: I never saw a boot that did not cover your ankle. It is a queer boot that would stop there.

* * * * *

Mr Hickey: It was poverty and starvation which gave Hitler his first start.

* * * * *

Dr Tubridy: . . . I have often wondered how Kerry people have so much 'coaxiorum'. . . .

* * * * *

Mr Hickey: . . . (An) expert of the British Air Force (says) that Foynes Air Port will play an important part in the next war. . . .

* * * * *

Mr Dillon: I offered you half a mountain in Wexford and you would not take it.

7. Snatches From Later Years

Mr Dockrell: . . . there is no such thing as a butter tree out of which you can make butter boxes or anything like that.

* * * * *

Mr Traynor: . . . I believe that no man in the L.D.F. at present will be without some piece of equipment.

* * * * *

General Mulcahy: Would the Minister say whether the bakers who supply the Army and the public authorities use yeast and salt and fuel and petrol. . . ?

* * * * *

Mr McDevitt: . . . if I were an able bodied fellow, I would prefer to be a turf-worker than a Deputy. . . .

* * * * *

Mr Lehane: . . . we should develop and advertise our Irish dishes and stand over them. . . .

* * * * *

Mr MacEntee: Deputy Sweetman had better give up pretending to be a cuckoo sitting on a mare's nest.

* * * * *

Mr McGrath: I do not know why people pay to hear Jimmy O'Dea when they can come here for nothing and hear you.

* * * * *

Mr Walsh: Who said that wheat was political?

* * * * *

Mr Cogan: Why do Irish writers concentrate so much on belittling their own people, degrading them as coarse, vulgar and brutal? Surely there are some educated, refined people in the country. . . .

Glossary

The extracts in this book are reproduced exactly as they appeared in the Official Report. Where deputies bearing similar surnames appear in the text of Dáil Reports, initials are given only in some cases. Therefore it is not always possible to identify positively who is speaking. The following alphabetical list may be of assistance.

Aiken, Frank
Alton, Ernest H. Prof.
Anthony, Richard
Bartley, Gerald
Baxter, Ptk F.
Beamish, Richard H.
Beckett, J. W.
Bennett, George C.
Benson, Ernest E.
Blythe, Ernest
Boland, Gerald,
Brady, Seán
Brennan, Ml
Briscoe, Robert
Brodrick, Seán
Burke, Jas A (Séamus de Burca)
Burke, J. M.
Byrne, Alfred
Byrne, C. M.
Carney Frank
Cassidy, Archie T.
Cleary, Ml
Coburn, Jas
Colahan, H.
Cole, W. L.
Concannon, Mrs H.
Conlon, J.
Cooney, Eamonn
Cooper, Major Bryan R.
Corish, Richard
Corry, Martin
Cosgrave, Philip

Cosgrave, W. T.
Costello, John A.
Craig, Sir James
Crowley, Fredrick H.
Crowley, Tadhg
Curran, Ptk
D'Alton, Louis J.
Daly, John
Davin, Wm
Davitt, Robert Emmet
de Bhulb, Seóirse
de Róiste, Liam
Derrig, Thos
de Valera, Eamon
Dillon, James M.
Dockrell, Henry M.
Donnelly, Eamon
Egan, B. M.
Egan, P. J.
Egan, M.
Esmond, Osmond G.
Everett, Jas
Fagan, Chas
Figgis, Darrell
Finlay, John
Fitzgerald, Desmond
Fitzgerald-Kenney, Jas
Flinn, Hugo
Flynn, Stephen
Fogarty, P. J.
Giles, Ptk Capt.
Gilligan, Ptk

Good, John
Gorey, D. J.
Hales, Thos
Hayes, Ml
Heffernan, Ml
Heron, Archie
Hewat, Wm
Hogan Connor
Hogan, Ptk
Hughes, P.
Johnson, T.
Jordan, M.
Jordan, Stephen
Keating, John
Kelly, Jas P.
Kelly, Thos
Kennedy, Hugh
Kent, David
Keogh, Myles
Keogh, Ptk
Keyes, Ml
Killilea, Mark
Lavery, Cecil
Law, Hugh A.
Lehane, Con
Lemass, Seán F.
Linehan, Timothy
Little, P. J.
Lynch, Fionán
Lyons, J.
McCabe, Alasdair
McCartan, Ptk
McDermot, Frank
McDevitt, H. A.
MacEntee, Seán
McGilligan, Ptk
MacGiobuin, Seán
McGowan, Gerald
McKenna, P.

McMenamin, Danl
Magennis, W. Prof.
Milroy, Seán
Minch, Sydney B.
Moore, Seamus
Morrissey, Danl
Mulcahy, Richard, General
Nolan, John T.
Norton, Wm
Ó Ceallaigh, Seán T.
O'Connell, T. J.
O'Driscoll, Margaret Collins, Mrs
O'Grady, Seán
O'Hanlon, John F.
O'Higgins, Brian
O'Higgins, Kevin
O'Higgins, Thos, Dr
Ó hÓgáin, Pádraig
O'Keefe, Ptk
O'Leary, Danl
Ó Máille, Pádraig
O'Neill, Eamonn
O'Sullivan, Gearóid
O'Sullivan, John M.
Redmond, Wm A. Capt
Rice, Vincent
Rogers, Ptk J.
Ryan, Jas Dr
Shaw. P. W.
Smith, Ptk
Tierney, Ml Prof.
Tubridy, Seán
Ua Buachalla, Domhnall
Vaughan, Danl
Victory, Jas
Walsh, Jas J.
Walsh, Richard
White, Vincent Dr
Wilson, Richard
Wolfe, George

THE BOOK OF IRISH WIT AND HUMOUR
Edited by Daniel O'Keeffe

A selection of sparkling Irish wit from the following authors:
Edward J. Delaney, John M. Feehan, James Stephens, Con O'Leary, Niall Sheridan, John D. Sheridan, Oscar Wilde, Canon Sheehan, Jonathan Swift, H. de Vere Stackpoole, E. Somerville and Martin Ross, Charles Lever, Lennox Robinson.

This is a genuinely funny book, a real tonic for the times in which we live; 128 pages of smiles, grins, roars, guffaws and mirth-provoking material. Never before have we been more in need of a laugh to save our sense of humour. We are introduced to a host of unforgettable characters who rollick and crash through the pages of this splendid book.

A hilarious book for the entire family to bring hours of enjoyment to everyone — ideal for your bedside table. The general reader will devour it for sheer delight. *The Book of Irish Wit and Humour* will be savoured by anyone who lays his or her hands on it.

HOW THE IRISH SPEAK ENGLISH
Padraic O'Farrell

How the Irish Speak English is a colourful and fascinating collection of the sayings and expressions which are still used by the Irish today. Padraic O'Farrell presents them leavened with folklore and local history and if they are sometimes extended into 'yarns' who will quibble? — for Irish wit and humour at their best are contained in eveyday anecdotes.

> Talk away — your tongue is no scandal
> That fellow would skin a flea for a ha'penny
> I was pushing an open door
> She had too much mileage up
> Run your lamps over that
> You won't tear in the plucking
> I'll give you Paddy Ryan's supper
> You'd see more flesh on a tinker's stick after a row
> I'll give you £5 and the run of your teeth

Little-known words such as 'schraums', 'kelters', 'grawls', 'gommerils' are explained within suitable contexts and the examples quoted help to illuminate the byways of 'Irish' English.